"MURDER'S A TOUGH BUSINESS"

The Pursuit of True Evil

INTRODUCTION

In the 1970's I was just beginning my law enforcement career and I was a huge fan of the TV crime series *Baretta*. *Robert Blake's* depiction of the street-tough detective dressed in jeans and short sleeve pullover shirts jumping over car hoods and slamming bad guys to the ground had me glued to the screen. His aggressive but compassionate attitude was right up my alley. *Baretta* could even be empathetic to the bad guys when the situation called for it. The philosophy was, "Don't Do The Crime If You Can't Do The Time!" Dig It.

It seemed to me murder was the most serious crime of all, so that's what I decided to concentrate on. Over the years I have worked almost every kind of killing you can imagine. From Saturday night beer joint killings to complex homicidal maniacs. I was privileged to study under such world renowned experts as Behavioral Science Unit Profiler Roy Hazlewood at the FBI National Academy. One of the most rewarding aspects of my career was working alongside and learning from some of the best investigators and prosecutors who ever lived, many of whom will be credited on the last pages of this work.

I also had the unique experience of facilitating training with literally thousands of officers over a 25 year stretch. We had the opportunity to discuss and analyze dozens, if not hundreds of homicide cases at length. The insight and knowledge shared in these sessions was invaluable to all of us.

Murder's A Tough Business is not meant to be a police report crammed with every minute detail of every case. Each case presented is defined with key points and issues I believe to be significant to illustrate how killers think and act and how they are caught and prosecuted.

There are several reasons real names are not always used in the book. In some murders, it is obvious the killer was seeking fame and notoriety. I am certainly not going to help them make a name for themself at the expense of innocent lives. In other cases, I do not want to unnecessarily drag up painful memories for people related to both victims and killers. Hopefully, they have been able, at least to some extent, put the past behind and go on with life. And finally, some committed the ultimate sin, paid their debt to society, and are trying to live the rest of their life as productive members of that society. I sincerely wish them the best.

I was once asked how I could have seen all that I have seen and still believe there is a God.

I firmly believe *pure evil* walks on this earth. I have peered deep into another human being's eyes and felt as though I was literally communicating with the devil. The feeling has been so strong I had chills run up and down my back. As a matter of fact it is happening now as I type these words.

There are also those who God has put in place to fight this evil. It is only by the love and grace of God that these forces have the will, strength, and determination to oppose the powerful demons who have existed since the beginning of our history. That is the ultimate proof there is a living God.

If you are an investigator and want to improve your skills, hopefully, *Murder's A Tough Business* will help you along your way.

On the other hand, if you enjoy reading *real stories written by real investigators* who did the work, hold on to your seat.
This book is the real deal!

Jim Leach
December 2020

"Jim and I worked together in law enforcement for years investigating some of the most hideous cases. I believe that Jim would use his best investigative skills as an author and produce a wonderful murder mystery. If you enjoy a great mystery with top-notch investigative work, be sure to read this book. Kudos to Mr. Leach, this is a great read." Sheriff Delphus V. Hicks Jr.

Legendary Sheriff Delphus Hicks served the people of Hardeman County as their Sheriff for 20 years. He was the first African-American to be elected Sheriff in the history of Tennessee.

SPECIAL THANKS TO ALL THE DEDICATED WOMEN AND MEN WHO WEAR THE BADGE AND PROTECT THE REST OF US FROM CHAOS

COVER DESIGN BY MR. STEVE POLLOCK

ISBN# 978-0-578-24879-0

Jim Leach's other great books are available at Amazon.com:

"You Can Tell ME, Effective Interviewing Made Simple"

"Not In OUR HOUSE" is a detailed manual designed to help businesses, government offices, and schools defeat the threat of workplace violence.

"Not In OUR SCHOOL" describes the violent issues we are facing in our schools and offers suggestions to help solve the problem.

Check out our website including blogs and podcasts at tugnews.com, or our You Tube Channel, "Tennessee Underground"!

What People Have Said About The Author

"There's always something new to learn from Jimmie Leach. Being able to draw from his extensive knowledge and expertise in investigation techniques is an asset to an investigator. I look forward to reading his latest book, "Murder's a Tough Business", and benefiting from Jimmie's insight into the depraved minds of killers, and deciphering their thoughts and actions."
SAC Terry Wolfe

State of Tennessee

Terry D. Wolfe

Special Agent in Charge (Retired)

Special Investigations Unit

" Jim Leach is well known for his ability to solve difficult murders. If you are interested in homicide investigations, his new book,

"Murder's A Tough Business" is a MUST READ." Sheriff David Woolfork

Former Sheriff David Woolfork served as the sheriff of Madison County Tennessee for 20 years, was honored by being the President of The Tennessee Sheriff's Association, and was the first African-American elected Sheriff in Madison County.

"Along the way, the author of "Murder's A Tough Business" and I worked together at the beginning of our careers as uniformed patrol officers. Then, again, years later when I was Chief Investigator for a Sheriff's Office and Jimmie was the TBI Agent assigned to that county.Our paths have crossed many times over the years in our profession and I am honored to have had his friendship over the years." Marshall Jeff Holt

Former U.S. Marshall Jeff Holt, a 45-year law enforcement veteran, served as a patrol officer, an Investigator, Chief of Police, and Sheriff. He holds a B.S. in Criminal Justice and graduated from the 159th Session of the FBI National Academy.

"Although these cases have been broadcast on local and/or national TV newscasts, having the insight of a career law enforcement investigator adds so much more to the story." Ellen Ramsey-Barr

Ellen Ramsey-Barr has retired from the corporate world and is now enjoying life in small-town America. She is an avid reader of mysteries, all things Amish, and enjoys studying different religions from around the world.

"I am eagerly waiting for the new book written by Jim Leach. He is extremely knowledgeable about criminals, particularly those who have committed murder. He

writes with the authority of experience and makes even horrible facts interesting."
Madeleine Russell

Madeleine Russell is retired from the University of Tennessee in Knoxville and is an avid reader. She has followed Mr. Leach's work for years.

THE CASES

WHAT HAVE YOU DONE TO MOMMY? - A mother and her two children are missing. The true story of what happened to them is one of the most horrible we have ever seen.

PLEASE STOP! - This case has to be one of the most coldly calculated, premeditated murders of all time. Page 38

THE KILLING OF AN NBA STAR - Lorenzen Wright as a multimillionaire professional basketball from Memphis. His young life ended when he became the victim of a murder. What happened?
This case has about every angle you can imagine in a murder!
Page 66

KELLY COCHRAN - Our podcast on Tennessee Underground described a murderous couple of serial killers who may have operated in Tennessee. Prompted by questions from one of our listeners, we looked a little deeper! Page 84

EXORCISM IN NEW MEXICO - A frail young man with a terrible illness had a father who became a religious zealot. Was the father serious about curing his son or was he a cult leader interested only in exerting his own dominance? Page 104

NO BODY! - This case involves money, love, and power. The problem is, where is the victim? How can you prosecute a murder case without a victim? Page 120

THE WRONG MAN? - NOT HARDLY!! - Check out this analysis of a discussion questioning the validity of a guilty plea to a vicious murder. Sometimes emotions may cloud the issues! Page 133

THE TRUTH, THE WHOLE TRUTH, AND NOTHING BUT THE TRUTH..REALLY?? - Two cold-blooded killers try and cover up the evil of what they did. A great study in body language and attempted deceit. To make it even better, jump on the internet and find videos of their interviews! Page 140

THE SANTA FE HIGH SCHOOL MURDERS - A 17 year old kills 10 and wounds 12 others.

Could these senseless murders have been prevented? Experts believe one of the reasons school killers commit their terrible acts is to become famous. We do not intend to help them gain notoriety, so we will not use their real names. Page 150 attempts to justify his murderous acts. Once again, the   killer's real name will not be used. Page 191

GOOD SHOT.. OR NOT? - When the police must take a life in the line of duty, a thorough investigation must be conducted. These are not *normal* cases and many factors must be considered. Here is what a seasoned investigator who has investigated *many* police shootings has to say.

IT WAS JIMMY B. - What do you do when a killer is identified through *very unusual means?*

IT'S JUST A LITTLE CUT - How much can a little blood evidence reveal?

YOUR BODY SPEAKS, BUT WHAT'S IT SAYING?

READING THE SCENE - What can a homicide scene tell you? Do dead men *really talk*?
Page 233

A DIFFERENT LIMB - Was a small mental hospital a treatment facility for those with minor issues or was it really a haven for some with more violent tendencies? A small southern town is devastated by fear of the unknown.
A small, unexpected development in the case ultimately provided the answer. Page 242

HOLLY BOBO - This tragic case involving the abduction of a young medical student shattered a peaceful existence in rural Tennessee. Follow the day to day account of this terribly complicated trial. Was justice served?
You decide for yourself. Page 253

THE GOLDEN STATE KILLER - One of the most interesting cases ever. The trail of terror stretched out for decades and touched over 10 counties in California. Come along with us and look into the mind of history's most unusual serial killers. Page 326

"WHAT HAVE YOU DONE TO MOMMY??"

In 1974 I was a young student at Ole Miss studying Criminal Justice. I remember being alone in my dorm room one night and I was immersed in Vincent Bugliosi's captivating book about the Manson Murders, "Helter Skelter". Simply put, it was terrifying. I locked my door.

I believe that experience was the dawning of my realization that fiction writers would never be able to compete with real life.

The town of Frederick Colorado had never experienced evil like this before.

When 34-year-old Shanann Watts and her two young children, Celeste, 3, and Bella, 4, were discovered missing on August 13th, 2018, several things were strange. Shana's car keys, purse, wallet, and cell phone were at home.

Her car was home as well the car seats for both babies.

Shanann had been out of town on a business trip and when she got back in town, her friend Nichole Atkinson gave her a ride from the airport and dropped her off at home at about 2 am on August 13th. Her husband, Chris was at home with the kids.

Nichole says Shanann, who was pregnant, missed an OB-GYN appointment and a business appointment later that day, and Shanann was not returning Nichole's text messages. When Nichole contacted Chris about where Shanann might be, he seemed unconcerned and said something about his wife being gone on a "play date" with other women. That seemed especially strange since this was the first day of school for the children. Nichole went to the Watt's home around noon but did not find Shanann at home. At that point, Nichole contacted the police who arrived at the Watts' home at 1:40 pm on August 13th.

Once police arrived they discovered the house was locked from the inside. Shanann's husband, Chris, got home soon after the police showed up and he had to use the garage door opener to let the police in the house. There was no reasonable explanation as to how a stranger could have gotten into the house, abducted the people inside, then left the house locked up. Someone would have had the garage door closer or been fast enough to hit the "close" button inside the garage, totally controlling the wife and two kids, and get out of the garage before the door closed.

Watts told police he and his wife were talking about selling the house. He told officers Shanann was taking the kids to a friend's house contradicting what he told Nichole. When he opened the garage door, the first thing he did was start looking through the car parked in the garage, not checking on his family. It was hard to believe Shanann was taking the kids somewhere since the car and both baby seats were still home. From what we now know, considering all he had just done, murdering his entire family, it is understandable he could have been a little confused.

Chris began giving TV media interviews the day after police became involved. He told reporters his last conversation with his wife before she disappeared " wasn't, like, an argument". Watts went on to describe the conversation as an "emotional conversation" and ended up by saying "I'll leave it at that". During the interviews, Watts seemed more focused on himself than his missing family. He talked about being lonely and said the house wasn't the same without his wife and children. He said he couldn't sleep. Watts stated more than once, "I don't know where she is", and said, "I could never fathom something like this happening".   In cases of this nature, one of the common characteristics of the perpetrator is to focus on themself.

Reporters have experience in conducting interviews and studying human behavior. The reporters present during this interview noted they saw no tears and no evidence of fear or anguish from Watts during the interview.

In viewing the interview on YouTube, the murderer was seen to have his arms crossed high on his chest in a defensive, closed body language posture. He exhibited inconsistent eye contact even to the point of slowly closing his eyes on several occasions while talking. Other signs of stress, nervousness, or guilt observed during the media interview included body swaying, nervous laughter, and excessive nose scratching.

Watts later failed a polygraph examination administered by police.

Police suspected foul play and looked for someone who had means, opportunity, and motive (M.O.M.). Even though the motive was not clear at this time, Watts had the means and opportunity to abduct his wife and two children. It was critical to the investigation that Chris Watts be cleared before investigators moved on to look at someone else.

When they began to question Watts, the killer told police several different stories. In his first statement to police, he admitted to having an emotional conversation with Shanann, and the point of contention was Chris's admitted infidelity. Watts said he told Shanann he wanted a separation, then he went downstairs. Chris claims he looked at the baby cam and saw their daughter Bella stretched out on the floor. The killer tried to put the blame on his wife by saying Bella had turned blue because Shanann had strangled the child to death. He goes on to say Shanann was in the process of strangling their other daughter Celeste when, Watts said, he went back upstairs. Watts claimed he flew into a rage, lost control of himself, and strangled his wife to death.

In a later interview, the murderer claimed Shanann threatened to divorce him and take the children. When faced with the threat of losing his children, Watts says he felt like something "snapped" inside of him. At this point, Watts admitted to strangling his wife to death.

Strangulation is a terribly vicious way to murder someone. According to experts, death by strangulation would probably have taken 2-4 minutes. The victim would be desperately struggling for air and panicking at the most extreme level imaginable until she blacked out. He would have continued to strangle her to make sure the job was done. Watts says his wife did not struggle. This is a preposterous lie. She would have been, literally, fighting for her life and the life of her unborn child.

Watts said while he was wrapping his wife's body up in a sheet in preparation for the disposal of her body, the children walked into the room.

One of the children said, **"What have you done to Mommy?"**.

The killer went on to say he loaded his wife's body into his truck. He also put his children in the truck and then drove to his worksite at Anadarko Petroleum. Words cannot express the horror the children must have experienced in the 45 minute drive from home to the worksite. When asked why he didn't just kill the children at home, he was unable to give any reason.

Upon reaching his work site he strangled Celeste while she sat next to her sister in the small truck cab. He then forced Celeste's dead body through a pipe and into a petroleum pit, and returned to his truck to kill Bella.

Of course, Bella had witnessed her sister being murdered and by this time she had to know her father had killed her mother. She begged her father not to kill her. Watts says the last words his daughter spoke were **"Daddy, NO!"** The medical examiner found evidence Bella fought back, but of course, she was overpowered. It appears as though she struggled so hard she bit through her tongue. Bella was also stuffed through a pipe and into a petroleum vat.

The monster used the same blanket to strangle both children. The pipes he forced them through were only 8" in diameter, so it must have been difficult to shove their little bodies through such a small opening. Remnants of hair and skin were recovered by police around the openings of the pipes. After killing Bella and Celeste and disposing of their bodies, Watts buried Shanann. Her body was found face down in a shallow grave. In his depraved mind, he may have buried Shannan face down so she wouldn't be looking at him from the grave.

In an effort to distance himself from the sheer evil of his act, Watts said maybe Shanann was praying for him while he murdered her. He tried to compare his murderous act with the crucifixion of Jesus Christ. Watts referred to Jesus asking God to forgive the people who were killing him and the killer speculated Shanann may have been asking God to forgive her murderer while he was killing her.

The killer *says*, now that he is in prison, he is reading the Bible every day. It seems many folks say they are reading the Bible frequently once they are incarcerated. This phenomenon is referred to as getting "Jailhouse Religion".

Watts says he did not plan the murder. He claims he asks himself the question, "did I know I was going to do that?" He goes on to say, "It just felt like there was already something... and I had no control over it." The killer says it was as if "other" hands were on top of his while he was choking the life out of his wife and those "other" hands wouldn't let him stop killing her. Watts went on to say it was like he had lost his mind and "didn't know what had happened."

In some of the cases we have been involved in, it is obvious some murderers attempt to lessen the cruel results of their acts by trying to blame someone or something else instead of accepting the blame themself. Tommy Lynn Sells who was convicted of 23 murders said, "sometimes the knife just goes crazy". Kenneth O'Guinn confessed to killing 5 women and said he murdered them because they reminded him of his wife who had been unfaithful to him. Walter Stitts who choked 2 people to death and tried to kill another attempted to excuse his murderous actions by saying the victims owed him money and refused to pay.

What Was The Motive?

Prosecutors say Chris Watts' motive must have been the killer's desire to establish a new life and give himself a fresh start.

In the past Shanann talked about how great Chris was and what a happy marriage the two enjoyed. On social media she seemed to be very happy, bragging on both her husband and the children. She said Chris was the motivator behind deciding to have a third child. Shanann was suffering from poor health when she first met her future husband. She is quoted as saying Watts "knew me at my worst", "he stuck around", and, "he is amazing".

More recently Shanann had begun to question her husband's fidelity. It turns out she was right. One of Shanann's friends said Shanann's was planning for the couple to separate

On a trip Shanann took to South Carolina to visit her parents, Chris showed up there for a brief visit. He was probably just making sure his wife would be gone from home for a while giving him a chance to see more of his girlfriend. Evidence revealed he did a lot of traveling with his girlfriend while his wife was in South Carolina. After he murdered his family, but before their bodies were discovered, Watts continued to text his girlfriend and talk about future vacations they could take together and what kind of jewelry he was going to buy for her. When the girlfriend found out about the murders, she came forward voluntarily. She had deleted many of the messages and videos that showed her relationship with the killer because she had decided to end the affair. Following a thorough investigation, authorities concluded there was no reason to believe Watts' girlfriend had prior knowledge or any involvement in the murders.

On top of the relationship changes, the Watts family had serious financial issues. They were forced to file bankruptcy in 2015. There were two savings accounts. One had a balance of less than $10, while the other account had a balance of less than $900. Monthly expenses included a $500 car payment and a $3,000 mortgage payment. On the very day Watts executed his family, the murderer mentioned to a neighbor he was considering selling the home. Adding to the financial pressure, there was a third child on the way.

The prosecutor discussed the cases with Shanann's family and there was a mutual agreement not to pursue the death penalty. Chris Watts was charged with 1 count of First Degree Murder as well as 2 counts of First Degree Murder of a Child Under the Age of 12 by a Person in a Position of Trust. Lesser charges included one count of Unlawful Termination of a Pregnancy in the First Degree and 3 counts of Tampering With a Deceased Human Body.

Watts quickly entered a guilty plea and received 3 consecutive life sentences plus 84 years on the murder charges. He has no opportunity for parole. He also pleaded guilty to other lesser crimes.

Key Issues

To build probable cause and decide how to interview a suspect, you must put together all the facts you know and determine what options are available. Below are some of the issues we thought were significant in this case.

The multiple stories Watts told to Nichole and police may be the foundation to begin to build probable cause. The different explanations of her whereabouts show a desire to deceive investigators. It also gives interviewers a possible approach to questioning that could create stress for Watts and make it more difficult for him to control his body language and overall demeanor.

Keep in mind, proving someone is a liar is not the same as proving someone committed murder!

In successive interviews with police, the killer progressed from having an "emotional conversation" with Shanann to saying his wife threatened to divorce him and take the children, and then he said he watched the baby cam as Shanann killed one of the children and began murdering the other child. He says he flew into a rage, lost control, and "snapped". He told police that he "had no control over it", and it was "like other hands were on top of his" when he was choking his family members to death.   All these descriptions are attempts to try and distance himself from the guilt and sheer, evil, cold-blooded nature of what he had done. Sometimes letting a suspect make it easier to talk about what happened can be beneficial. Never forget. The object is to get truthful information, not to make him feel bad, OR make YOU feel superior in some way.

When faced with this type of interviewing situation, an interviewer must decide on what approach will work best in trying to question a person exhibiting these emotions. It is tremendously important to remember the objective of the interview is to get the other person to open up and talk to you. The interviewer must make a judgment as to what approach, or theme, is best suited to produce this result.

Broadly speaking, there are two ways to go about it. The interviewer can empathize with the suspect and make him think you understand what he did and why he did it, or you can try stressing him by emphasizing the seriousness of what he has done. It is a judgment call as to which tactic should be used. If you see the approach you are using is not working, then change your approach! Usually, it is easier to switch from an understanding approach to a hard nosed theme than to go from hard-nosed approach to trying to be "a good guy".

Successfully conducting an interview like this is an art, not a science.

It seems every story Watts told mentioned his marital infidelity. This may indicate that the conversation did actually happen and was weighing heavily on his mind and could be used in questioning him.

In TV interviews Watts wanted to emphasize how much HE had been hurt by the absence of his family. This may have been an attempt to divert attention from the fact that his family was gone and unaccounted for and probably in his sick way of thinking, he may have thought HE could gain sympathy because of all HE had been through. A normal, innocent person would probably show more concern for his missing family than for himself. Watts is obviously a totally self-centered person.

Watts eventually confessed when he found out he couldn't beat the polygraph. There is an excellent video of the polygraph session in the HLN Lies, Crime, and Video documentary series. The episode aired on 7/13/19 and was titled "Killer Dad, Chris Watts Speaks".

Apparently, police suspected the bodies might have been disposed of at Watt's worksite because the area was placed under surveillance by police. If he had not confessed, the investigative question might have arisen as to whether or not police should give him a ride out to the site while they were questioning him. Taking a suspect back to the scene might cause enough of an emotional reaction that he will confess. Caution must be exercised to guard against allegations of coercion.

If you carry him back to the scene, it would be appropriate to ask what he talked to the children about on the ride. They knew he had killed their mother. If you were trying to empathize with Watts, you might suggest he was still trying to figure out what to do with the kids. Didn't really want to kill them. On the other hand, it would be a good time to point out what a cold-blooded killer he was.

An important point to understand. Chris Watts was obviously the prime suspect for several reasons we have already discussed. Investigators must do as much as possible to either "put him in, or put him out" before moving on to another suspect. In some cases, this can be difficult. In a very high profile case, the murder of Jon Benet Ramsey, years were spent discussing the guilt or innocence of her parents before they were proclaimed innocent.

In such a terrible crime, does the motive matter? Yes. The judge and jury want to hear it.

PLEASE STOP!

Cheryl Berreth reported her daughter, Kelsey Berreth, missing on December 2, 2018. Cheryl had received a text from Kelsey's phone two days after Thanksgiving. The text message said Kelsey would give Cheryl a phone call the next day. That call never came.

Kelsey, a 29-year-old mother, disappeared on Thanksgiving Day, November 22, 2018. Kelsey's one year old daughter, Kaylee, was with her father, Kelsey's fiance, Patrick Frazee.

Kelsey's boss received a text on November 25th that came from Kelsey's phone saying her grandmother was sick and she would be off work for a week. The boss received this text in response to one he sent to all employees wishing them a happy holiday. He had also received a text from Kelsey's phone on Thanksgiving Day that he said appeared to be strange. The punctuation did not match the way Kelsey normally wrote her texts and there was no smiley face where she usually placed one.

Kelsey's brother, Clint, said he tried to text her several times the week after Thanksgiving but got no reply. He had bought Kaylee a Christmas ornament and wanted to see if it had been delivered. The police found the package on the doorstep when they first performed a welfare check at Kelsey's condo.

Cheryl Berreth said Patrick told her he and Kelsey had broken up because she wanted "her space". Cheryl had not heard anything of this nature from her daughter. Kelsey and Frazee never actually lived together during their relationship.

Cheryl asked Frazee to check Kelsey's condo but he said he needed to go check on some cattle. Cheryl said she doesn't know if Patrick ever went to the condo to check on Kelsey.

Concerned about Kelsey, Cheryl and Clint traveled from their home in Washington to Colorado and visited

Kelsey's condo. Cheryl had a key to the apartment. The home gave the appearance of someone who left unexpectedly. Uncovered cinnamon rolls were sitting on the stove. Kelsey's luggage, make-up, and toiletries were still in the condo. Cheryl and Clint spent a long time talking to the police after seeing the condition of Kelsey's condo. When Clint later reported, what he believed to be blood, under the bowl of the toilet, police asked them to leave the apartment so no evidence would be accidentally contaminated.

Investigators asked Cheryl and Clint if they had used any cleaning supplies in the condo. Cheryl replied they had only used dishwashing detergent to clean the dishes. This means if police discover the presence of cleaning agents in the condo, it is evidence someone may have tried to clean up the crime scene.

By December 21st when it became obvious the condo might be a murder scene, police searches became more intense.

Police searches and inquiries were conducted to see if Kelsey had taken a trip or was simply traveling. No trip plans, gas purchases, ATM withdrawals, etc.. were found in searching her laptop or bank records. This evidence was not consistent with someone voluntarily leaving their home.

When police first questioned Patrick, he said he had last seen Kelsey on November 24th when he said he returned her car, gun, and house keys to her. Upon searching the condo, police found none of these items.

Patrick also mentioned Kelsey had been to rehab for depression and alcohol abuse. Police found no evidence of this treatment.

Frazee told police he received a text saying Kelsey's phone had expired on November 29th.

The whole time police were questioning him, Frazee never asked about Kelsey's whereabouts or any leads police had uncovered. Indeed, some people act differently than others in a crisis situation, but according to several witnesses, Patrick appeared to be totally unconcerned about Kelsey.

When they searched Frazee's apartment, police found handwritten notes detailing Patrick's movements on November 22nd. These notes almost read like a police report and they even included times for each of his movements. This one-day diary may have been an attempt to establish an alibi. No other reason comes to mind as to why he would make such notes for this particular day. He probably never thought investigators would uncover the notes!

There were also ATM receipts for November 22nd showing 5 deposits and one withdrawal.

Why so many visits to the ATM, especially on Thanksgiving Day? Once again, one explanation could be he was attempting to create an alibi.

There was also a receipt from Walmart on the 22nd at 1:50 p.m., a November bank statement for a bank account in Frazee's name, and a Waste Management receipt for household trash dump, a quantity of 70 yards, stamped on 12/1/18 at 12:39 p.m. Items related to child custody issues were also recovered from Frazee's home.

Credit Union records show the last transaction on Kelsey's account was on the same day at Safeway. Security video confirms Kelsey and Kaylee were at the Safeway.

Frazee came into the bank on December 5th and asked for photos of his visit to the ATM on the 22nd. His stated reason for needing the photo was to establish a timeline for himself on that day. He told bank employees he and Kelsey had broken up and there was going to be a dispute about child custody. The manager grew suspicious and contacted the bank's legal advisers as well as the police. She felt strongly enough about her encounter with Frazee that she made notes about what had transpired. She also thought it was strange Frazee showed no concern for Kelsey or their daughter.

A Verizon store manager said Frazee came to the store on December 11th and asked questions about how someone might access his cell phone account and if information could be obtained even though the phone was destroyed. Frazee said he wanted to change the PIN on his phone but gave no explanation concerning what happened to the other phone. When the manager, Mr. Felis, told him the corporate office would have to be contacted, Frazee became upset. When the corporate office was contacted they said they could not help with changing the PIN either, even though Frazee said he needed to change the number for "security" reasons. The Verizon manager was concerned due to the way Frazee was behaving and contacted police about the conversation. Frazee also told him not to believe the things that were being said about him (Frazee).

Investigators found a call on Frazee's cell phone made between 4:30 p.m. and 4:40 p.m. on November 22nd, Thanksgiving Day, to an Idaho number. The number belonged to Patrick's girlfriend, Krystal Lee Kenney!

Digital records from a surveillance camera with a view of Kelsey's front door. The camera showed 4 instances of movement on November 21st and 27 instances of movement on November 22nd. . Of the twenty seven images which were captured from the camera on November 22nd Frazee was seen in 11 of them. Photos of Kelsey entering her home with a baby carrier were taken at 3:54 a.m. on the 22nd and one at 11:56 a.m. shows her at the door. An image around noon on the 22nd shows Frazee preparing to enter the condo. At 1:23 p.m. the camera captured Kelsey, Frazee, and the baby entering the condo. Berreth was carrying flowers and the baby carrier. This is the last known picture of Kelsey at the condo.

Timeline of some significant events:

4/18   Frazee tells a friend of a plan to kill Kelsey. Frazee uses the phrase, "No Body, no crime".

11/22   Thanksgiving Day
   Kelsey disappears.
   Frazee makes 5 deposits,1 withdrawal at ATM.
   Frazee has a receipt from Walmart, 1:50 pm.
   Frazee makes a call to his girlfriend in Idaho, 4:30 pm.
   The surveillance camera at Kelsey's condo goes off 27 times.

11/24   Mother gets a text from Kelsey's phone.

11/25   Kelsey's boss gets a text saying Kelsey is taking a week off.

12/3   Last known location of Kelsey's phone. It was near Krystal Kenney's home in Idaho.

12/4   Mother and brother go to Kelsey's home. They found blood behind the toilet.

12/5   Frazee makes a strange visit to the bank.

12/11 Frazee makes another unusual visit, this time to Verizon.

Frazee was charged with two counts of first degree murder, three counts of solicitation to commit murder, two counts of a crime of violence, and one count of tampering with a body.

The Trial

During the trial defense attorneys pointed out there were no pictures of Frazee holding a large black tote even though prosecutors insisted he took Kelsey's body out of the condo in a black tote. There is much testimony about various cameras capturing images of both Kelsey and Frazee.

The prosecution points to a video that appears to show a black tote of some type in the back of Frazee's truck. After he makes the last known trip to Kelsey's condo, it looks like the tote is in a different position. The prosecution contends that the tote is in a different position because Frazee has put Kelsey's body in the tote.

Frazee tells police he received a text from Kelsey a couple of days after Thanksgiving. According to Frazee, the text said, "Do you even love me?" Frazee says he tried to return the text but it didn't go through.

Police checked with Verizon and the last known location of Kelsey's phone was in Gooding Idaho on December 3rd at 5:13 p.m. This is near the home of Frazee's girlfriend, Krystal Lee Kenney.

Kenney initially lied to the FBI but eventually became a witness.

Krystal says Frazee gave her Kelsey's phone and told her to go far away and text Kelsey's mother and boss. Krystal also turned over to police a pistol Frazee had given her and it was traced back to Kelsey. Frazee told police he gave the gun back to Kelsey.

Krystal goes on to say Frazee tried to talk her into murdering Kelsey.

According to the girlfriend, Frazee attempted to use his daughter as the reason his fiance should be killed. Krystal says Frazee told her that his daughter was in "imminent danger" while in her mother's care and if the child was harmed, it would be Kenney's fault if she refused to commit the murder.

Frazee told many people Kelsey mistreated Kaylee and that Kelsey was undergoing treatment for substance abuse. The investigation showed neither of these allegations was true.

Kenney testified Frazee told her to give Kelsey drugged coffee, then gave her a pipe to hit Kelsey in the head, and finally, he gave her a baseball bat and told her to, "swing away". Kenney went as far as going to Kelsey's house at one point but a barking dog scared her away. She finally told Frazee she couldn't do it.

Krystal alleges when she wouldn't commit the murder, Frazee did it himself.

Kenney says Frazee told her he beat Kelsey to death with a baseball bat.

A search of Frazee's property revealed a tooth fragment that a forensic anthropologist testified was "probably human". Another specialist said there was not enough DNA on the tooth fragment to make a positive match with another person, but the tests indicated the DNA on the tooth belonged to a woman. Other small pieces of tooth or bone were found during the search, but there was not enough substance for DNA testing. This evidence would seem to corroborate the story of a bludgeoning death which could knock the teeth fragments out of the victim's mouth. More evidence would come later.

Krystal says she received a call from Frazee on Thanksgiving Day and he seemed upset. He told her there was a mess to clean up and he needed her help. When she arrived in Colorado Frazee told her to go to Kelsey's home and start cleaning it up.

Ms. Kenney says there was blood everywhere.

Kelsey's parents visited the condo on December 4th and noticed film from cleaning supplies were in several places in the apartment including on the furniture, TV, stove, and other places.

Tests were performed at the home later and the results indicated the presence of blood containing Kelsey's DNA, in the bathroom around the toilet, bathtub, and the towel rack. Blood in these areas would be consistent with someone trying to clean themself up after attempting to clean the crime scene.

Kenney testified Frazee told her Kelsey's body was "in a tote" in the back of his truck. She saw the tote, but never looked inside it to see if there was actually a body in the tote or not. She goes on to say she and Frazee took the tote to a ranch he was leasing, poured gas on top of it, set the container on fire, and burned it. She says Frazee told her the tote burned all night.

It takes a long time and a hot fire to burn up a human body.

A cadaver dog alerted in the area Kenney pointed out as the spot where the tote was burned, but the officer handling the dog could not testify he was *positive* the dog's alert was because of a decomposing body.

Many times when experts testify in court, they *feel* certain something is a fact, however, they can't *prove* it to be a fact therefore they can't *testify* to it in such a way. It is good investigative technique to always go and talk to forensic experts. They may say what they think that will not be in the report because they can't prove it. *Their thoughts can provide valuable investigative leads!*

Video footage was viewed in court that showed Kenney and Frazee filling up a gas can and placing it in the bed of the truck which tends to back up the witness's testimony.

A friend of Frazee's, Joseph Paul Moore testified Frazee told him in April of 2018 he had figured out a way to kill Kelsey. When Moore told Frazee he shouldn't say things like that, according to Moore, Frazee said, "No body, no crime, right?"

Frazee's brother, Sean, who is a police officer, was called as a prosecution witness. He said Patrick Frazee had lived with their mother on the family ranch for 20 years. At the family Thanksgiving dinner, Patrick was late showing up. Patrick showed up with his daughter, Kaylee. about 5 p.m. and made some food for himself and his child. It should be noted, the family is fighting over the father's $400,000 estate and Patrick and Sean haven't talked in 2-3 years.

The first time Sean heard Kelsey was missing was when Patrick told him about her disappearance in a phone call on December 3rd. Patrick told Sean that Kelsey's grandmother was sick and Kelsey may have gone to visit her grandmother. He also told Sean that Kelsey was having issues concerning dependency and she could have gone for treatment without telling anybody. Patrick went on to say Kelsey's work had called about canceling her insurance due to her absence from work. When Sean was released from the witness stand her looked at Patrick and rolled his eyes!

Several of Kelsey's co-workers testified they had been concerned about Kelsey. She suffered from the stress of a very high-pressure job as well as having an infant child to rear. Contrary to what Patrick Frazee told several people, Kelsey's friends saw no evidence of her having any problems with drugs or alcohol and there was absolutely no evidence of baby Kaylee being mistreated. When asked, Kelsey's co-workers said in their opinion, she would never desert her child.

A person from the Human Resource Department at Kelsey's work told the court that at one time Patrick Frazee was the beneficiary of Kelsey's life insurance policy but it is unclear if the policy is still in effect. Would Frazee have been under the impression he stood to receive the proceeds of an insurance policy if "something" happened to Kelsey?

On the last day of prosecution testimony, the state dropped a couple of bombshells.

An expert in bloodstain pattern analysis and crime scene reconstruction, Denver Police Officer Jonathyn Priest, testified about the blood spatters and drops in Kelsey Berreth's condo. He said the pattern of stains discovered in her condo would be consistent with what would be seen with a person being bludgeoned 10-15 times with a baseball bat. Priest explained the first blow would open up the wound and subsequent strikes would have splattered the blood. Kenney had testified earlier there were bloody footprints in the bathroom and on the floor of the second floor loft. Priest said that would mean a person stepped in a "relatively significant source of blood."

When asked about the blood spatters on appliances, counters, and high up on the walls, Officer Priest explained the blood would splatter in an arc and the force of the strike would determine the length of the arc. In other words, the harder the strike, the farther the blood would splatter.

The expert testified the blood on the toilet was a "transfer stain" meaning something had touched blood elsewhere and then touched the toilet. Blood on the couch showed wipe marks which indicated someone had tried to clean it up.

Defense attorneys pointed out the fact that many of Priest's opinions were drawn from what Kenney said she saw. The officer said that was true. On redirect examination, prosecutors pointed out there were no inconsistencies between Kenney's testimony and Priest's conclusions.

A former inmate who lived in the same "pod" (a living area for inmates) with Frazee testified Patrick tried to get him to kill witnesses who planned to testify against Patrick Frazee. The inmate initially asked to remain anonymous and even though some media outlets identified him, we will not identify him by his real name. He feared retaliation from prison gangs simply because he cooperated with law enforcement. We will call him Jim.

Jim received a reduction in the charges he was facing and the defense suggested prosecutors were involved in having Jim's charges reduced in return for his cooperation. Jim said he did even know the charges had been reduced when he came forward with the information, but he admitted he hoped for a better plea agreement if he cooperated. No one at the prosecution table was involved in the plea bargain deal Jim received. There was no indication the inmate was influenced to twist his story in exchange for leniency.

Frazee asked about a tattoo on Jim's face. The tattoo represented membership in a prison gang, but Jim said he no longer belonged to the gang. Frazee offered to help get Jim bonded out of jail if Jim would help murder some witnesses.

Jim gave police letters he received while he was in jail and there is an assumption the letters came from Frazee. Jim says they came from Frazee, Agent Slater said it looked like Frazee's handwriting, and the story the letters present closely resembles the facts surrounding the disappearance and murder of Kelsey Berreth. Especially the part about sending text messages from a victim's phone after they are dead. That sounds pretty familiar! The letters were captioned by Patrick Frazee as, "instruction or suggestions to carry out the hits so to speak on the witnesses."

Jim's testimony was bolstered by CBI (Colorado Bureau of Investigation) Agent Gregg Slater who reviewed 17 letters between Jim and Frazee in reference to killing Krystal Kenney (Frazee girlfriend and accomplice), Chad Lee, Michelle Stein (friend of Kenney), John Moore (friend of Frazee who testified against him), and Wendi Clark (friend of Moore. Frazee referred to her as a "cash cow"). In the letters, Frazee explained all the people needed to disappear, at least until November 22, or whenever the trial is over. In one letter Frazee said he would, "really like to see Kenney with a bullet in her head".

In letter #12, Frazee said, "Kidnap and hide 'em until you're done. South Florissant (Frazee's hometown). Guy and chick. 55-60 years old." This is supposedly a reference to John Moore and Wendi Clark.

Letter #14 asks, "Do you have funds or resources to go to Idaho and back? Was thinking if you cap 'em in the desert," Agent Slater said this would have been in reference to Kenney and Stein.

In letter #15 an interesting suggestion is made by the letter writer. "I'm excited if we can pull this off - only thing better would be if Krystal *sent someone a text from her phone and confessing that I didn't have anything to do with it at all.* Greg Slater and all 5 disappear." The end of this message, "all five disappear", was said to refer to Kenney's family. Including the children.

The letters contained instructions to flush them down the toilet once they were read. Obviously, these instructions were ignored.

The defense did not cross examine Slater.

The prosecution rested after the presentation of this witness.

The defense offered no proof.

Attorneys made their closing arguments and the case was given to the jury for deliberation.

It took the jury only 3 hours to convict Patrick Frazee on every count.

This is very quick and probably means the jury convicted on the first vote. Years ago we had a sheriff charged with 172 counts in federal court. The jury voted guilty on all charges and did it so quickly, they waited a while before reporting they had reached a verdict. The foreman of the jury told prosecutors after the trial, jurors were afraid if they reported as soon as they finished voting, it would give the appearance they had not given the case enough consideration!

Prosecutors decided before the trial not to seek the death penalty.

Patrick Frazee was sentenced to life plus 156 years without the possibility of parole.

Krystal Lee Kenney pled guilty to a charge of tampering with evidence and she received a 3 year sentence. Of course, her sentencing was deferred until the trial was over to ensure she delivered truthful testimony.

Young Kaylee is in the custody of Kelsey's parents.

Key Issues

When you prosecute a murder case without the victim's body, obviously there are issues you must confront. You must: A) Prove the victim is dead, B) Prove the death was not the result of natural causes, and C) The accused caused the death.

The prosecution may use either witness testimony, physical evidence, direct evidence, or any combination of the three depending on the circumstances of the case and the evidence available. To receive a guilty verdict, the prosecution must prove ALL elements of the crime(s) the defendant is charged with.

In this case, the State did an excellent job of tying the evidence together and showing a consistent theory that the jury obviously believed. Even the inmate letters suggested a method of operation that mirrored Kelsey's murder. Kelsey's body was disposed of and her cell phone was used after her death to try and confuse investigators working on the case.

The DNA, blood spatter evidence, cell phone records, and surveillance video corroborated the story of the main prosecution witness, Krystal Lee Kenney. Investigators did a good job of using interview questions and investigative techniques to give meaning to the circumstantial evidence.

The prosecution did a good job of ruling out other scenarios. When trying a case in which the evidence is primarily circumstantial, it is important to demonstrate to the jury that the prosecution's theory of how the crime happened is the only "reasonable" explanation.

The more evidence investigators have accumulated, the greater the chance they will be able to conduct productive interviews. We were interviewing a man who had strangled two people to death and at the beginning of the interview, he attempted to deny the fact he had anything to do with the murders. When investigators interrupted his denials and pointed out all the evidence against him, he realized the futility of lying and confessed to both murders.

Remember, even if the accused confesses or makes a strong admission of guilt, you must do everything possible to corroborate what he says. Assume he will try to "take it back" and defense attorneys will try and say investigators told the killer what to say, "lead" him, or participated in other improper techniques.

Police and prosecutors also did a great job of anticipating defense issues and having answers for their questions before the questions were even brought up.

Investigators performed a good follow up investigation when Patrick gave statements. It was proven he lied and this fact could have probably been used if he tried to take the witness stand and testify on his own behalf. No matter what the judge says in his charge to the jury, jurors would really like to hear the defendant say he "didn't do it". This type of information might also help prove Frazee was not out of his mind. He was cold blooded and calculating.

Officer Priest did an excellent job on the witness stand. The defense tried to upset him by saying many of his expert opinions were based on another person's (Kenney) observations. They probably hoped Officer Priest would become defensive, but he was too smart for that! He simply agreed with the defense attorneys and the prosecutors followed up by emphasizing Kenney's testimony and Priest's testimony were totally consistent with one another.

When Frazee was describing the murder to his girlfriend, he said Kelsey's last words were, "Please stop".

KILLING OF AN NBA STAR

Former NBA and University of Memphis basketball star Lorenzen Wright was murdered near Memphis Tennessee in July of 2010. Wright was 34 years old and had been out of professional basketball for about a year after playing 13 years in the NBA.

On December 16, 2017, Memphis Police Director Mike Rallings announced that Wrights' ex-wife Sherra Wright-Robinson and Billy Turner had been arrested on charges involving conspiracy to commit first-degree murder. Sherra was arrested in Riverside California. Turner is a resident of Collierville Tennessee, a suburb of Memphis, and was arrested locally. Both remain in jail on very high bonds. The Director would not elaborate on the evidence.

At the time of his death, Wright was living in Atlanta but had come to Collierville to visit his children. A friend says he dropped Lorenzen off at his former wife's house at 10 p.m. on July 17, 2010. Wright told his friend he would call him later to come and pick him up. Wright told his friend that Sherra insisted he come to her house that night. According to the friend, he never received that call from Wright to come and pick him up.

In Sherra's first statement to police, she said her former husband ran out of her house that night and she never saw him again. In a later interview, she stated Lorenzen left with a box full of drugs and he said he was "going to flip" something for $120,000. She further related two unknown men had been stalking the former basketball star.

A call was placed to Germantown 911 from Lorenzen Wright's phone at 12:05 a.m. the next morning. The call was interrupted by gunfire in the background, eleven shots in all.

Nine days after his disappearance Wright's body was found in a field near

Hack's Cross Road and Winchester Road in Memphis after police located the cell phone tower the 911 call was transmitted from. The weather had decomposed the body to some extent. It was determined by forensic experts he was shot five times by two different guns. Shell casings were found at the scene where the body was found. Of course, this would indicate semi-automatic (or automatic) weapons were used and possibly multiple shooters. The casings also seem to say the murder occurred at the scene where the body was found. Lorenzen was hit twice in his skull, twice in the chest, and once in his right forearm. The victim's watch and other jewelry were still on his body, possibly indicating this was not a robbery.

On an interesting note, Sherra Wright -Robinson wrote a fictional novel titled, "Mr. Tell Me Anything". The *fictional* work tells the story of a woman, Sharon Roberson, who is married to an NBA player (sound familiar?) and describes the basketball player as a womanizer who finally gets serious about another (younger) woman. Media reports say Lorenzen had a younger girlfriend when he and Wright-Robinson finally divorced. Sherra said the book was based on her life with Lorenzen and even indicated she was going to write a follow-up novel in which the NBA star would be killed!

In a media interview in 2010, Sherra discussed her financial problems. Following her former husband's death, she received one million dollars from a life insurance Lorenzen had taken out as a stipulation in the divorce. Sherra also received a large sum of money from an NBA pension plan. The money was supposed to be spent on expenses related to the couple's children. Supposedly the money was spent in about ten months.

The victims' assistant, Wendy Wilson, remembers receiving threatening messages from Sherra in the early 2000s. Ms. Wilson is quoted as saying the messages " were very disconcerting, threatening in nature. Very off-key. She (Sherra) was very jealous and very, very insecure".   According to Wilson, Sherra said if she ever caught him (Lorenzen) with anyone else she would kill him. Ms. Wilson gave tapes of the messages to the police.

The investigation also revealed Lorenzen was in bad financial shape himself. Apparently, he sold two luxury cars to a man with extensive drug connections, but the DEA found no indication the victim was involved with the drug business. The evidence indicates it was strictly a deal to sell two expensive cars to raise some money. A lot of dope dealers like fancy cars!

About seven years after the murder, Jimmie Martin, who was in prison for murder, told authorities he had helped Billy Ray and Sherra clean up the crime scene and accompanied Turner to the lake in Mississippi where Turner threw the gun. He is a cousin to Sherra Wright.

Martin, who is 35 years old, is serving a 20 year sentence for murdering his girlfriend. He was acquitted of First Degree Murder in 2009 and was out on bond awaiting his next trial when Lorenzo Wright was killed. Martin goes on to say he was involved in an unsuccessful attempt to murder Lorenzen in Atlanta. Martin says that attempt was spoiled when the attackers climbed through an open window and found an unknown man sleeping on the couch in Lorenzen's home.

Jimmie Martin told police he was at a meeting with Sherra Wright, Billy Turner, and a third person when the murder of Lorenzen was planned. The investigation discovered the third person to be Claudia Robinson. It is unclear how much of a role Claudia played in the murder. Prosecutors have only referred to her as being present at the meeting. She has not been charged.

Martin confirms the motive for the murder was the insurance money. A few days after the murder, Sherra came to Mississippi and got Jimmie to help clean up the crime scene. Sherra borrowed a metal detector from Martin's mother to help find and destroy evidence. Apparently, in all the excitement of the confrontation and murder, somebody dropped one of the guns used to kill Lorenzen. The gun was found with the aid of the metal detector and Butler and Martin threw it in the lake in Mississippi. Jimmie Martin told the police where the gun was located and that is when investigators found the weapon. Martin says he received "payment" for his part in the murder, but it is unclear what the payment amounted to.

Butler and Sherra were placed under electronic surveillance by the police following the discovery of the murder weapon and investigators listened as the pair discussed the discovery of the evidence. The suspects speculated on the fact that an informant was involved. Later. Sherra flew to Memphis from California and met with Billy Ray. Police observed and documented the meeting with photographs of the two together.

TRIAL ISSUES

Similar to the Holley Bobo case, the credibility of an informant witness who is also a co-conspirator will be one of the main issues in the trial. Defense attorneys have already called Jimmie Martin a convicted murderer and a liar. They claim Martin lied forty times in his own murder trial!

It is not clear what motivated Jimmie Martin to come forward with the information seven years after the fact. Several possibilities exist. Perhaps the police had discovered information tying him to the crime and when confronted, Jimmie decided he better cut a deal. There could be some kind of personal reason, such as a family illness, that made Martin want to cut a deal and get out of jail as soon as possible. It could be that after several years of incarceration Martin grew a conscience and sought to relieve some guilt.

The important point is for police and prosecutors to know what his *real motivation* is and be prepared to present that motive to a jury in a way that the jury can accept it. Notice we emphasized *real motivation*. The real motivation may be different from what the witness told police. Many times the defense may know what the *real* motive is and it is different from what the witness told prosecutors. In this situation, if the defense surprises the prosecution by divulging the true motive during the trial, it can make prosecutors and investigators look either deceitful or incompetent and either one can be devastating to the prosecution's case! It is hard to see how the case can be tried without putting Martin on the witness stand to testify.

Is Jimmie Martin a liar? You bet he is! Everybody lies. The question prosecutors have to answer will be, **is he lying about the facts of this case?** It is important that any testimony Martin gives that can be corroborated, *is corroborated*. Can police establish if there was a guy on Lorenzen's couch when Martin and Turner supposedly attempted to kill the basketball star? Will Claudia Robinson back up what Martin says about the planning meeting? Of course, if she cut a deal to testify, she has may have a credibility problem.

Where is the second gun? The forensic specialists say two guns were used. As far as we know, only one has been recovered. It is not necessarily a fact, but the evidence of two guns being used may indicate more than one shooter. If so, who was the second shooter? Sherra? Martin?

There are probably other issues that have not been released to the media. Corroboration of ANY of these issues could enhance Martin's credibility as a witness

Was there any evidence *at all* there were other suspects? If so, were they totally cleared of involvement? No matter how flimsy the evidence, a good defense attorney may capitalize on leads like this to confuse a jury!

Is there any chance Billy Ray or Sherra might try to make a deal? The prosecutor may believe the case is good enough without another principal witness, in which case, probably no more deals will be made. On the other hand, if Billy Ray or Sherra agree to testify, it could take away the need for a long and costly trial because the other defendant may decide it is futile to go to trial and fight the case!

There will probably be discussion about the phone call and meeting between Turner and Wright. Did Sherra sound fearful after the murder weapon was found, or was she only interested because it dealt with her former husband's death? Did she and Turner try to have a "secret" meeting, or were they just getting together because they were friends? If the jury views photographs of the meeting, what kind of body language and physical demeanor are they going to see?

The defense may try to say Martin is the actual killer, but this could be tricky. In order to use this technique, they just about have to admit their own client had, at least, some involvement in the crime to come to the conclusion Martin was the killer! How could Billy Ray or Sherra have any pertinent information if they weren't involved?

Is it possible Sherra told the truth about Lorenzen doing a deal to make $120,00? The defense may say robbers could have killed him for the money and left the jewelry to disguise the fact a robbery occurred. A good attorney might attempt to plant this seed in juror's minds to create reasonable doubt. A good, detailed follow-up investigation on this story could destroy its credibility.

The two unknown men who were supposedly stalking Lorenzen deserve more attention. How did Sherra know about the men? Did she see them? What did they look like?   What made her think they were stalking Wright? She might simply say Lorenzen told her the story, but many times, if people are fabricating a story, they may add details to the lie in hopes that will make them more believable. If she is lying, the details may get them confused and trip them up when they are asked to tell the story more than once. The addition of details also gives investigators leads to either prove or disprove and may divulge a possible alibi.

A lot is dependent upon whether or not either of the defendants decides to talk. Every attempt should be made to stipulate in any plea agreement a full confession will be given.

Investigative Issues

Could you use the book Sherra has written as evidence against her in the murder trial? Probably not, unless she takes the witness stand in her defense or maybe it can show a theme or scheme that fits the crime. Even though the book seems to outline a plan to commit the murder that eventually took place, it does not *directly prove* she planned or participated in the crime! It may give investigators confidence they are "on the right track" and if Sherra takes the witness stand, prosecutors may be able to question her about writing the book and give the jury the benefit of that information. Investigators should go ahead and gather all possible information, get the information to the prosecutor, and let the prosecutor decide how best to use the information.

Prosecutors and investigators should try and prove any financial problems Sherra may have had **and** the fact that *she knew about the insurance.* Proving the insurance policy was in place may not prove too much in the courtroom. The important evidence would be she *knew the insurance existed and she could receive the money if Lorenzen was dead.* The insurance means nothing as evidence unless it can be shown as a motive to kill the victim!

Does it matter whether or not the victim was involved in the drug business? Unless defense attorneys argue drugs were the motive or in some way the reason for his murder, it probably won't matter. Having said that, investigators must gather all available information and provide it to prosecutors. A victim's history of illegal acts may influence a jury if they are allowed to hear it.

Make absolutely sure Martin COULD physically have been present and wasn't somewhere else! Begin by checking his driver's license or criminal history. If he got a speeding ticket 1000 miles away or was locked up on the day of the crime, he couldn't have been there when the crime happened. Make sure the records are accurate and it is the right person! Repeat this investigative technique with every witness to prepare a good, prosecutable case.

In this case, you would at least want to check on everyone who was supposed to be at "the meeting". This is very simple and basic investigative technique, but it can make a lot of difference in a successful prosecution. It can also keep the prosecution from being embarrassed. Think about getting in court and the defense attorney proves your star witness was in jail in San Diego when he says he saw something happen in Memphis.

Ascertain exactly how much involvement Martin had in the murder. Many times a witness will only tell you what they *think you know!* They fear if they tell you *everything,* it may result in it in more charges. Press Martin to make sure he was not MORE involved.

Find out more about the unknown man sleeping in Lorenzen Wright's home. You will not know *what he might know* until you talk to him.

Try and firm up the metal detector story!

Supposedly the discovered gun had been lost by the killers. Why would they take a chance on going back and looking for it? Is this why a second gun was used? Jurors will want to know the answer to these types of questions!

If the two defendants decide to turn state's evidence, how do you decide who you would rather deal with? Assume at some point one will try and put more blame on the other one! Who has the most culpability as opposed to who has the most information? Which one will be the best witness? The criminal record of any witness may affect how much credibility the jury attaches to their testimony, so the potential witness's history must be taken into account.

The original blog on this case was written in June 2018.

In July of 2019, Sherra Wright-Robinson pleaded guilty to Facilitation of First Degree Murder and Facilitation of a Criminal Attempt to

Commit First Degree Murder. She was sentenced to 30 years in prison.
Turner is still awaiting trial.

KELLY COCHRAN

In 2016 Kelly Cochran pleaded guilty in Indiana to killing her husband, Jason Cochran, and received a sentence of 65 years. This murder took place 2 years after she and Jason partnered to kill her lover Chris Regan.

At the time she entered the plea for the murder of her husband, she was already serving a sentence of life without parole from a jury trial in 2014 for killing her boyfriend, Chris Regan.

There was a time lapse of 16 months between the two killings.

After reviewing media coverage of these cases, which portrayed Jason and Kelly as serial killers and implied they killed someone in Tennessee, Steve Bowers and Jim Leach discussed the cases on their podcast, *Tennessee Underground.*

Several things were said to indicate the couple may have had tendencies similar to people who are serial offenders. Some allegations included suspicions of multiple murders committed because of unusual motivations, cannibalistic activities, and victims spread out over a large area and a long period of time.

After hearing our podcast, one of our favorite podcast participants shared her insightful observations. Hopefully, her questions, along with some other issues, are addressed in this blog.

- Question: *Looking at Kelly Cochran's mug shot, she shows no remorse or fear. Her demeanor almost seems to say she is proud of what she did. How does what she did not bother her?*

The look on her face could be the result of several different things.

It could be as simple as the person taking the picture was "flirting" with her!

It's hard for normal people to understand, but some people who do things that are too horrible to imagine, such as overdosing her husband with heroin and then smothering him to death, are actually proud of what they have done. There is a video, probably on YouTube, showing David Rader, the BTK Killer (Bind, Torture, and Kill) describing his actions in court during part of his plea agreement. It is obvious he enjoys describing the murders he committed. More than once, when explaining why he did certain things, he proudly said, "We serial killers". Sickening.

   Terri O'Donnell, the girlfriend of Chris Regan, described the look on Kelly Cochran's face in court as saying, "Look at what I did...You can't stop me.."
   Terri's observation brings to mind a definition of body language that says, "The body does what the mind is thinking"

- *Question: How does one serial killer meet and marry another serial killer?*

   In this particular case, if in fact, these two are actually serial killers, they met in high school.

Relationships may sometimes begin in prison between cellmates or other prisoners. Of course, these relationships would primarily be same sex because of the prison environment. However, cellmates or friends may have significant others on the outside who end becoming involved because of common interests.

However, a relationship between two serial offenders can begin in all kinds of different ways, much like normal people. If you think about it, we all tend to migrate toward people who have interests similar to our own.

Keep in mind a person does not just wake up one morning and decide to be a serial killer! It is an evolutionary process. Two people might not be killers when they first meet but desires for excitement, gratification, a curiosity of the unknown, dominance, sadism, or other feelings tempt them to experiment with new things and eventually drive them toward murder.

There are all kinds of groups and associations that bring together people of common interests.

Are you interested in sadism, masochism, pedophilia, necrophilia, cannibalism? Look around and you can find groups with similar interests and feelings. These groups have their own websites, chat rooms, etc...

● *Question: What has Kelly had to say?*

According to Kelly, she and Jason had an agreement with one another declaring they would kill anyone who became involved in an affair with either one of them. However, in sworn testimony (not that being under oath necessarily meant a lot to her!) she said the "pact" between them to kill any boyfriends or girlfriends was not serious. She considered it a joke. She also says Jason knew about her affair with Regan and was okay with it. Apparently, Kelly also had an affair with another one of her co-workers, a guy named Eric, and there was no attempt to kill Eric.

Kelly says Jason told her he would kill her if she was unfaithful!

Kelly said the relationship with her husband began with the two feeling like "soul mates" but ended up filled with verbal abuse and threats of physical violence.

Kelly says Jason once talked about killing her and then committing suicide. Sometimes someone who is in the frame of mind to kill themself may be very close to being ready to kill someone else!

Remember, she told all these things *AFTER* Jason was dead. There was no way he could rebut what she said! We only have Kelly's word to rely on. And that's not much...

One of the few things Kelly said that could be corroborated centered around the disposing of Chris's body. She said she and Jason cut the body up and threw it away in garbage bags. She led police to the site and evidence was recovered that backed up her story. Disgusting. No conscience.

What about Kelly Cochran's credibility?

What all did she lie about? First of all, she was found guilty of lying to the police about murder, dismembering a body, and disposing of evidence.

In the trial, Kelly said her husband killed Chris Regan without her knowledge and all she did was help get rid of the body.

She claimed Jason abused her and at one point held a gun to her head. The murdering Mrs. Cochran told police she was afraid not to help Jason.

She said Regan's remains were put in bags and thrown away near Crystal Falls Township, not far from Iron River. After confessing, Kelly took the police to the area where Regan's body was disposed of. They found Regan's skull with a bullet hole, glasses, and human bones. This, once again, is one of the few statements Kelly made that could be corroborated.

According to Kelly, her husband Jason, supposedly kept a "Trophy Bag" or a "Trinket Bag" containing *souvenirs* he collected when he committed all these other murders. Absolutely no evidence was uncovered to corroborate this statement by Kelly.

While in jail awaiting trial, Kelly wrote a letter to a newspaper. Several psychiatrists analyzed the letter and they all reached the same conclusions. The doctors said she showed signs of being a "self-pity narcissist", and she showed absolutely no remorse. The diagnosis went on to say she wished to write her own narrative. When she began to confess, she asked the detective if he was a good writer. She was enjoying the attention, even if it was the result of a terrible murder she committed.

Cochran said she only made claims of being a serial killer to make herself appear to be a MONSTER to get some sympathy from a jury. Do WHAT?? Juries are filled with smart, conscientious people. We don't understand how Kelly thought presenting herself as a cold blooded killer was going to engender sympathy from a jury. The jury gave her life without parole. How's that for sympathy Kelly?

Kelly's statements about being a serial killer *were* admitted in trial and then she tried to use this as a reason to appeal her conviction! She contended reciting her own words prejudiced the jury. Guess she shouldn't have said those things!

The appellate court ruled the prosecution only introduced her statements to show how Kelly tried to manipulate the police.

- Question: *Did Kelly and Jason suffer from emotional trauma or mental issues?*

At one point Jason told police he had been hearing voices. He had a documented history of mental and emotional issues. Regardless of anything Kelly says about Jason being unconcerned with the affair she was having, he killed the guy. No mention of a robbery or other motive. Sounds like it may have bothered him a little bit.

It goes without saying, Jason was obviously a dangerous individual.

We find no mention of outstanding mental or emotional trauma in Kelly's childhood. As an adult, she voluntarily admitted herself into a psychiatric hospital and was diagnosed as having "Suicidal Ideation". While in jail she made threats of violence and suicide.

Let's try and separate fact from fiction. Were these folks serial killers or not?

Many times after the arrest or conviction, more information comes forward from various sources. Sometimes the credibility of this information is questionable! People tend to come forward and sort of say, "I could have told you so". Maybe they think it makes them look smart or knowledgeable. Perhaps they are seeking, "15 minutes of fame". In many instances, people may be trying to aid the investigation but accidentally present their beliefs or suppositions as fact.

Kelly's brother Colton Gaboyan says he believes she killed at least 9 more people and has committed murder in Michigan, Indiana, Minnesota, and Tennessee.

What evidence did he see or hear that made him draw this conclusion? We don't know of any evidence!

Then there's the story about dismembering the victim (which apparently happened), grilling the human remains and feeding the neighbors at a cookout (which apparently DIDN'T happen). The news that the Cochran's murdered Regan caused folks to start talking.

You can almost hear the reasoning (gossip!). "You remember when they had that cookout? They didn't have the money to buy all that meat! You don't reckon..?". "When they were grilling that meat for us, didn't you think it smelled strange? I wonder what human flesh smells like when it is cooked?". "They had to get rid of the body some way!". "One night I heard a noise coming from their house that sounded like somebody sawing something", "I heard that too!"

And there you have it. It makes an interesting story and people with the behavioral characteristics of a serial killer do, in fact, many times practice cannibalism. This may give an excellent example an excellent of a little trick our brain plays on us sometimes.

Let's say we see "A" and "C" happen. Our knowledge, experience, and perception combine all we know with what we saw, heard, felt, smelled, or tasted. Then our brain tells us that, "If "A" and "C" happened, then "B" MUST have happened too". In fact "B" DID NOT really happen, but we believe it did because our brain has told us it did!

Without speculation by the neighbors concerning the cookout and claims Kelly made about killing more people, along with her brother's speculation, there would probably no mention of "serial killers" in this case.

● Question: *How many people did the murderous couple really kill?*

Former Iron River Police Chief Laura Frizzo said Kelly spoke of killing 21 people, but the Chief thought it was probably 5. Colton Gaboyan, Kelly's brother says the death total is 9. The investigator who took her confession thinks she killed more than 2.

According to speculation from Kelly's brother, Colton, the murders stretched across Tennessee, Minnesota, Michigan, and Indiana. The only places where murders have been discovered and proof exists the Cochran's were involved are Michigan and Indiana. Kelly was arrested in Kentucky. Of course, investigators may have more information that has not yet been released.

Sometimes a person may tell you they committed other crimes, but they don't or *can't* supply enough information for you to follow up.

We were involved in the investigation of a multiple-victim killer. Two murders and one attempted murder could be proven. He said he had killed 5 people but could not give enough information to locate all the bodies, or even be sure in what jurisdiction the crimes were committed.

In our investigation, the killer was picking victims he just happened to come across as opposed to the method of operation the Cochrans practiced. From what we know, the Cochrans killed people they *knew* in an area they were *familiar* with. If that is the case, Kelly should be able to give credible information, if she is telling the truth.

Kelly clearly enjoys the limelight. She has already been sentenced to prison for life. Most places would agree to no death penalty for these types of murders if the crimes could be cleared up and the families given some closure. Indiana has already made that stipulation. If she has committed other murders, why not go ahead and confess? Kelly is already serving a sentence of life without parole, so, another sentence is really no big deal!

Perhaps she is not confessing because she *can't*! There is a huge difference between saying, "I killed 21 people" and confessing to a murder. To confess, you must know some *facts.*

A lot of law enforcement agencies learned this lesson the hard way many years ago when dealing with Henry Lee Lucas and Odis Toole. These two pretty much confessed to any murder they were questioned about and too often investigators took them at their word. Once police (and news reporters) starting looking into Lucas and Toole's statements, they found a few problems. Such as when the pair would confess to a murder in Arizona, we'll say, and they were in jail in Florida at the time the crime was committed!

- *The question remains, were Kelly and Jason serial killers, or just mean?*

Several possible scenarios could explain the murder of Chris Regan.

First and foremost, always make sure the K.I.S.S. method doesn't give you the answer! K.I.S.S. stands for Keep It Simple Stupid, Ha! If you completely rule out the most simple, basic theory, then you can move on to something else. You can't always totally be successful at ruling out the obvious answer, but investigate it as thoroughly as you can. Don't take a case with a simple answer and make it complicated!

Let's consider some possible scenarios that might result in the motivation to kill.

Scenario #1. Jason caught Kelly messing around. Perhaps she thought Jason would be gone from home and invited Regan over. This would a very daring move, but it would also be more exciting! Too bad it backfired when Jason unexpectedly stayed or returned home. Imagine her surprise... Jason shot Regan and forced Kelly to help him dispose of the body.

    Scenario #2. Jason finds out about Chris Regan and tells Kelly *somebody has to go.* It could either be Kelly or Chris. Kelly decides it needs to be Regan instead of Kelly. She invites Regan to come over with the intent of killing him. Probably safe to assume they robbed him too although no evidence of a robbery is mentioned. Lack of evidence does always mean an absence of guilt.

    Scenario #3. Jason was gone so Kelly invited Regan to come to the house. Something happened once he got to their home and *Kelly killed him!* Jason helped dispose of the body.

    Scenario #4. Robbery gone bad

    Scenario #5. Dope deal gone bad

    Scenario #6. The Cochrans were, in fact, serial killers

Scenarios numbers 1-5 are responsible for a whole lot more murders than scenario number 6!

Why would Kelly kill Jason?

Reason #1. He was the only witness that could tie Kelly into the murder of Chris Regan

Reason #2. The two lovebirds had a falling out over something. It could have been anything. It is probably a good bet Kelly was one to hold a grudge!

Reason #3. This *ideal marriage* may have been falling apart. They were involved in a murder together, they were both drug abusers, and they both had mental issues. Sounds like there could have been a little stress on the home front and stress can often result in violence!

Reason #4. Kelly was not a nice person.

Reason #5. Kelly found a new lover.

Reason #6. Kelly says she just couldn't forgive Jason for murdering her *true love,* Chris. Whatever...

KEY ISSUES

➤ There is no proof we are aware of that more than two murders were committed by this pair, either together or apart.

➤ There are several normal, easy to understand motives that cause these two murders to happen.

➤ Judging by the available evidence, Chris Regan's body was dismembered and disposed of in an area away from the murder scene. Kelly Cochran led police to the area and significant evidence was recovered to corroborate her story. There is nothing to support the story that the victim's body was fed to neighbors.

➤ Kelly Cochran admits she lied about killing a bunch of people. It should be noted she freely described the killing of her boyfriend and her husband. If she had killed others, she would probably enjoy talking about those crimes, too.

❖ You might want to see a documentary titled *Dead North* describing these cases on the Investigative Discovery Channel. The short series is predominately narrated by the former Chief of Police Iron River Michigan Laura Frizzo.

EXORCISM IN NEW MEXICO

The Amalia Compound raid in Taos county New Mexico was initiated on August 3rd 2018 when one of the women in the compound frantically sent out a message asking for help because the people in Amalia Compound were starving.

As a result of the raid, 11 children were placed in protective custody, 3 women and 2 men were arrested. One of the men arrested was Siraj Ibn Wahhaj, the father of Abdul Ghani Wahhaj and one of the leaders of the cult. The other man arrested was Wahhaj's brother-in-law, Lucas Morten. Two of the women were Siraj Ibn's sisters, Hujrah Wahhaj and Subhanah, who is also Lucas Morten's wife.

The third woman arrested was Jany Leveille from Haiti who was described as Siraj Ibn's "Muslim wife". She was identified by the teenagers as the "leader" of the group. The adults were initially charged with child abuse.

Accounts from those familiar with the situation described the inhabitants as "near starvation" and "living like they were in a third world country". When asked who owned the land one of the men replied, "The Lord gave it to us." During the initial raid on the compound police found weapons, extra magazines for the firearms, and a bullet-resistant vest. The suspects had built a firing range on the property.

Three year old Abdul-Ghani-Wahhaj was reported missing from his home in Georgia months before the raid. The child's mother Halima Ramzi said her son and his father, Siraj Ibn Wahhaj, left her home in Georgia to go to a park and never returned.

When questioned, Wahhaj stalled his wife by saying he just wanted his son to spend the night with him. At the time Ramzi and Siraj were married but she filed for divorce in December. The young child suffered from hypoxic ischemic encephalopathy, an affliction that caused him to have seizures. The disease required constant medical care and treatment.

Prosecutors say Wahhaj and his accomplices believed they were going to heal the child by practicing certain religious ceremonies. According to state and federal court documents, Wahhaj returned from a trip to Saudi Arabia in October 2017 and announced that medical treatments for his son were to be stopped and that he (Wahhaj) would perform certain rituals to "cast demonic spirits" out of the child's body.

The "treatments" began in Georgia but Janey Leveille said she had been commanded by the angel Gabriel to take the child to New Mexico to continue their mission. She kept a personal journal describing how she could interpret messages from God. The journal also documents the death of little Abdul Ghanni Wahhaj. Janey contacted another one of Siraj's brothers and asked him to join the group in New Mexico and become a martyr. The mention of martyrdom seems to indicate she understood the nature of their plans.

The children say the rituals performed on the child lasted for several days and during the ceremonies, Wahhaj would recite verses from the Qur'an and keep his hand on his son's forehead while the father was praying. The children say the sick child was foaming at the mouth while his father was performing one of the attempted exorcisms. The child subsequently lost consciousness and died.   His decomposing body has been identified from human remains discovered in a tunnel at the compound

The adults preached that young Wahhaj would be resurrected as Jesus four months after his death.

The leaders directed the members to be prepared to attack certain groups and institutions. From information gained through the investigation, prosecutors say the target list likely included schools, law enforcement, and financial institutions.

One of the teenagers is quoted as saying the children at the compound were told by their adult captors that any of the children who did not say they "believe the message" would be killed or kept hostage until they agreed to support the cause.

In Court...

Defense attorneys contended that if the defendants were white Christians instead of black Muslims, their actions would have been accepted as normal behavior. They said shooting guns on private property or believing in faith healing would not have been a problem! Evidently, the questions of starving children and making a 3-year-old child choke to death, possibly on his own vomit, were not considered bad behavior by these lawyers.

Local Judge Sarah Backus said the prosecution had not shown (to the judge's satisfaction) that the defendants were a threat or exactly what their plan was. (What more evidence could you have shown? What could happen if they are released?) The judge allowed the defendants to have unsecured bonds but for a while, all defendants remained in jail. The state of Georgia eventually declined to issue a fugitive warrant for Siraj Wahhaj. Apparently, officials in Georgia saw no need to issue a fugitive warrant since the charges in New Mexico would supersede the Georgia warrants.

In an interview with reporters, Jany Leveille's brother, Von Chelet Leveille, who still lives in Haiti, also says Siraj Wahhaj visited a faith healer in London to try and discover new remedies for his son's illness. Leveille is quoted as saying his sister told him the child died while his father was performing a meditative Islamic healing ritual called *ruqya*. The ruqya ritual is supposed to summon *jinn* (supernatural creatures) and demons by invoking the names of God and command them to stop their harmful activities. Some describe ruqya as a form of Islamic exorcism.

Von Chelet claims he learned of the boy's death last winter. He was having daily conversations with his sister in New Mexico using "WhatsApp". He was told the child's dead body was stored in a tunnel, washed frequently, and showed little signs of decomposition for quite some time. Von Chelet Leveille said the group trained with firearms as a self defense measure because the adult members feared public outrage when the child was resurrected as a black, Muslim child who was declared to be Jesus Christ.

State charges were dropped against the defendants because of the "10 day rule" which is a rule that requires the prosecution to give the arrested person a hearing within 10 days of their arraignment. This hearing places the burden of proof on the government to show there is enough evidence against the suspect to proceed with prosecution. It is many time referred to as a "preliminary hearing". The procedure helps to ensure the arrested person receives a reasonably speedy trial as guaranteed in the law. In many situations, the case is carried straight to the Grand Jury and an indictment is sought against the suspect. If the Grand Jury issues an indictment, it may circumvent the necessity for a preliminary hearing unless the defendant requests one. On September 7th indictments were issued against Siraj and Janey in state court. The couple is charged with "Abuse of a Child Resulting in Death". If convicted they could be sentenced to life in prison.

It appears the prosecution, in this case, may rely on testimony from children. Perhaps the state did not want to have a preliminary hearing because of the stress testifying in court would place on children who had already had to live through a tremendously traumatic experience. If the case goes to trial (it probably won't), the state will attempt to corroborate any testimony a child may give with other, independent evidence or officer testimony. Defense attorneys must be cautious with aggressive cross examination attacking a child witness because those types of tactics could be perceived as "bullying" and alienate jurors. In the end, the credibility of the person testifying is what matters, not their age.

On March 13, 2019, a federal grand jury in Albuquerque indicted Janey Leveille, Siraj Ibn, Hujrah Wahhaj, Subhanah Wahhaj, and Lucas Morton on several conspiracy charges centered around terroristic acts. Authorities say they will not pursue the death penalty. Federal court documents quote one of the teens as saying Siraj wanted to "get an army together" and prepare the 11 children for jihad. The children's training included "firearm, military techniques, rapid reloads and hand-to-hand combat". Extremist training literature was also discovered at the compound. Leveille told them "jihad" meant they were supposed to kill those who did not believe in Allah.

Everyone pleaded not guilty.

Leveille has been living in the U.S. illegally for 20 years arriving here in 1998 on a temporary visa. Reports say she wanted to marry Siraj Ibn so that she could become a United States citizen. Allegedly Leveille became pregnant but lost the child. She said the father of the child was Wahhaj and Leveille claimed she lost the child because of a voodoo curse cast by Wahhaj's wife. Leveille applied for permanent citizen status in May of 2017 but was turned down. If convicted on any of the charges, she will serve any prison sentence she receives first and then be deported back to Haiti.

Siraj Ibn's father, Siraj Wahhaj, was an unindicted co-conspirator in the bombing of the World Trade Center in New York City in 1993. In the ensuing criminal trial, the senior Wahhaj testified as a character witness for Sheik Omar Abdel Rahman, the blind sheik who was convicted of plotting the World Trade Center terror attacks. Siraj Wahhaj currently serves as an imam at a mosque in New York City. The imam says he helped to lead the authorities to the compound.

KEY ISSUES

The Sheriff said the compound had been under surveillance since May but law enforcement lacked enough evidence to search the property. The FBI was .watching the compound from the air using drones. The landowners gave the Sheriff permission to search the property but since the residents were the ones who had an expectation of privacy, without consent from the occupants, law enforcement was concerned that if they moved too quickly any evidence obtained as the result of the raid (search) might be inadmissible in court.

Authorities obviously wanted to get on the property and see what was going on sooner than they did. Their concerns about moving before they had enough information were legitimate. If you should be faced with a similar situation, you may need to try and "think outside the box". Sometimes probable cause must be achieved by an accumulation of circumstantial evidence. Compare this process with building a brick wall. Every time you add a brick (a bit of evidence), you make the wall (affidavit showing probable cause) stronger! Depending on the situation, evidence gathering might be bolstered by aerial surveillance using aircraft or drones. Electronic eavesdropping is valuable in the right circumstance. Interview anyone you can find who has been on the property. As a last resort, you might consider asking their permission but keep in mind this may give the suspects a chance to destroy evidence or threaten witnesses.

Of course, when gathering information to use in affidavits for search warrants or arrest warrants in a case of this nature, the law regarding separation of church and state could become an issue.

In questioning people involved in the group two approaches appear obvious. The group claimed to be religion based and you might be able to appeal to a group member's conscience by emphasizing the child's death and the mistreatment of ALL the children. Eventually, a juvenile court judge issued an arrest warrant for Wahhaj for failing to let Ramzi know where the child was located. Could the warrant have been used to gain access?

The other interviewing theme could be one of the "old standby's". The question is, "Do you want to be a witness or a defendant? Today is the day to decide." Of course you must be careful not to cross the line and be threatening or coercive. Keep in mind such things as your volume, tone of voice, and how close you get to the person you are questioning. Also, remember an investigator does not have the authority to make any promises about leniency. It is okay to say you will make their cooperation known to the prosecutor. Explaining the circumstances is not a *threat*.

The *deception* Siraj Ibn Wahhaj used to get his child away from the mother could be used to prove that Wahhaj knew what he was planning on doing was WRONG. Any testimony showing Wahhaj was aware his son might die without proper medical attention would be tremendously important. While proving motive or intent may not be an element of some crimes, jurors want to hear it!

In some cases, a decision must be made where prosecution should take place. In some cases, state court may have tougher sentencing laws, and in other cases, the federal system may be more strict. Federal conspiracy laws can be very broad and allow you to include "bit players" who might not be subject to being charged in state court. Once charged, these defendants may understand it is to their advantage to become a witness in exchange for some leniency.

Much of this case may rest on the testimony of children who have through terribly traumatic experiences. If properly questioned and prepared children can make excellent witnesses. Every attempt should be made to corroborate children's statements not only to prove the truthfulness and accuracy of the information but also to take some pressure off them when they testify in court. Whenever possible, ask child witnesses to compare what they are telling you to something that is *known*. For instance, if a child is describing a vehicle, ride them through a mall parking lot and have them show you a vehicle(s) similar to the one they are describing. The same technique may be used to describe colors, size, etc... This tactic might also open the door to getting the child off the witness stand letting the officer testify.

As we said earlier, these kids have been through a lot of trauma, so their mental and emotional well being must be of paramount importance. The less they have to testify or tell the story, the better unless mental health experts decide it is therapeutic for them to talk about their experience. Defense attorneys had best tread lightly when exposing the child witness to cross examination. A jury could be alienated very quickly if they perceive the child is being "bullied".

Lucas Morten has been diagnosed as incompetent to stand trial and is undergoing treatment.

Doctors say Janey Leveille is suffering from mental illness.

Siraj Ibn Wahhaj, Hujrah Wahhaj, and Subhanah Wahhaj all remain in custody.

NO BODY!

On May 24th of 2019, Jennifer Dulos disappeared from her New Canaan Connecticut home after dropping her kids off at school at 8:00 am. She missed some scheduled appointments that day and did not answer text messages or phone calls. Her purse was left in the house. Jennifer's vehicle was found a few miles away from her home.

Jennifer and her husband, Fotis Dulos, were going through a *very* heated divorce.

Along with other problems, there were financial issues involved in the dispute. Even though he appeared to be a successful real estate developer, authorities believe Fotis amassed $7 million in debt. The couple's 5 children, each had a trust of $2 million each ($10 million total). For him to be able to access the money, Fotis had to have custody of the children.

To further complicate matters Fotis was in litigation with the estate of

Jennifer's father regarding a 1.5 million dollar lawsuit. The lawsuit alleges the father-in-law loaned Fotis the money. Dulos now says the money was a *gift* from a loving father-in-law and not a loan.

The investigation discovered cell phone records indicating Fotis was heading in the direction of their home (Jennifer was living in the house) the morning of the disappearance. Fotis's blood was found mixed with Jennifer's blood on a kitchen faucet. Dulos's blood found in a house he had lived in might be easily explained. But when it is mixed with Jennifer's blood, on the kitchen faucet, and there are signs the scene was "cleaned up", Fotis's blood takes on a different meaning!

His DNA was also found on a doorknob in the kitchen. Blood spatters found at the home were analyzed by experts and the pattern seems to indicate a violent attack.

There was evidence the house had been thoroughly cleaned. For example, the housekeeper had left a dozen rolls of paper towels the night before and only two rolls were left.

On the day Jennifer disappeared, surveillance video showed Fotis and his girlfriend, Michelle Truconis, dumping bags in trash cans 75 miles away from home. The bags contained clothing, a sponge, a clear poncho, and 4 zip ties. Ms. Dulos's blood and DNA were found on over a dozen items including the zip ties. Police think the zip ties were used to tie Jennifer Dulos's hands while she was brutally murdered.

Mr. Dulos borrowed a Toyota truck from an employee on the day before the disappearance.

Fotis's friend Kent Mawhinney gets in the picture!

The 52 year old Fotis Dulos was a real estate developer and Kent Mawhinney was the closing attorney on many of Dulos's real estate deals. It seems their relationship went a little further than real estate transactions.

On the day before Jennifer's disappearance (5/23), Fotis had some kind of a gathering at his house at Jefferson Crossing. He left his house at 4:54 pm and transported the Toyota truck to a nearby house owned by his company. He was only gone 15 minutes.

Ten minutes after Fotis arrived back home, Fotis's fiend Kent Mawhinney's phone pinged near where Fotis had left the Toyota truck. Kent's phone pinged twice there, the last time at 5:23 pm. The investigation further revealed Fotis left home again at 5:35 pm and traveled to the area where the Toyota was located. He stayed there for 6 minutes.

On 5/24 (the day of the disappearance), Mawhinney arrived at Fotis's house at 7:30 am and stayed until 8:30 am. Fotis's phone alarm went off at 4:20 am.

Mawhinney first told police he was not at the house that morning, but when he was interviewed a second time, he admitted he was at Fotis's house that morning for a "business meeting". Apparently, he admitted being at Fotis's house after being confronted with cell phone records. When questioned, Troconis said both Fotis and Mawhinney were at the house that morning. She later admitted she never saw Fotis there that morning.

Fotis called Mawhinney at 7:47 pm and this is the same time video cameras show Fotis and Troconis throwing the bloody bags in the trash.

Police theorize on 5/24 Fotis loaded a bicycle in the truck, drove to New Canaan, and parked near the spot where Jennifer's vehicle was recovered.

On the same day, a video from the area of Jennifer's vehicle shows a person wearing a hoodie and riding a bicycle headed toward the Dulos home. The bicycle was similar to one owned by Fotis.

Before returning the truck to the owner, Mr. Dulos had it washed and detailed. This was verified by Ms.

Troconis's statement to police and also surveillance camera footage.

Fotis explained to the truck owner the seats in the truck needed to be replaced and Dulos offered to pay for the new seats. The owner later switched the seats but he saved the old seats and ended up giving them to the police. Jennifer Dulos's blood was present on one of the seats.

During the investigation police found a license plate belonging to Fotis in a drainage pipe in front of a bakery. This was in the same area as the trash cans where evidence was dumped. Once again, this was 75 miles from the crime scene. The plate had been altered to make identification more difficult.

Evidence of planning?

On 5/18 (6 days before Jennifer's disappearance) two people discovered a large hole, 6 feet long and 3.5 feet deep on the property of a gun club Mawhinney was affiliated with. The hole had been camouflaged by placing 2 barbecue grill grates that were partially covered with leaves and branches over the top. Inside the whole was a blue tarp and 2 bags of lime. Four days later the same two people returned to the hole and discovered it was half full of water and the lime was gone! The hole had been covered much better this time.

Perhaps Mawhinney got word of the discovery from some of his buddies in the gun club and figured plans should change. On the other hand, maybe the pair came up with a better idea of how to dispose of the body. It appears significant the lime was gone. Lime has been used in other cases to decompose a body.

Police dug up the hole and brought in cadaver dogs, but no human remains were discovered.

Ms. Troconis told investigators she and Fotis made up alibis and police found the notes full of their ideas. Investigators referred to their notes concerning possible alibis as "alibi scripts".

What else was the pair planning?

According to the arrest warrant, police said Mawhinney and Fotis Dulos were close friends, but Mawhinney's estranged wife Zelotes, speaking through her attorney, tells a different story. She says Fotis was not a close family friend. She alleges Fotis left her several voice messages asking her to meet with him on the pretext of helping her to "mend" her marriage. When she finally met with Fotis in a restaurant, he tried to talk her into going with him to his home in Farmington Connecticut to meet with Kent. She refused the invitation.

Zelotes filed a criminal complaint against Kent Mawhinney saying he violated a protective order she had against him by having Dulos contact her.

Kent had been arrested for sexual assault against Zelotes. She thinks Dulos was "indebted" to Mr. Mawhinney. Ms. Mawhinney now believes Fotis and Kent were planning to kill her if they could lure her to the Farmington house.

Key Issues

- Jennifer and Fotis Dulos were involved in a nasty divorce.

- Fotis Dulos was party to a civil suit with Jennifer's father's estate. The issue in the case was whether or not the money Fotis received from his father-in-law was a *loan or a gift!* If the court decided it was a loan, Dulos would have to pay the estate at least $1.5 million.

- If Fotis could gain custody of the children, he stood to get his hands on $10 million. No more money problems!

- Dulos borrowed a truck from one of his employees and used the borrowed truck and his bicycle to the house where Jennifer now lived by herself.

- Police believe he tied her up with zip ties, killed her, attempted to clean up the crime scene, and then disposed of evidence. Witness testimony, cell phone records, surveillance video, and forensic tests corroborate these police conclusions.

- Jennifer Dulos's body was not found. When Fotis returned the truck he used the day of her disappearance, he acted so unusual the truck owner turned over the truck seats to police. Police recovered Jennifer's DNA from the truck seats.

- Fotis actually made "alibi scripts". His mistake was, he had his girlfriend, Michelle Truconis help him. She eventually cooperated with police and investigators ended up with the notes.

Results of the investigation

All the combined circumstantial evidence was shown to The state's chief medical examiner, Dr. James R. Gill. According to the affidavit filed with the warrant, Dr. Gill concluded Ms. Dulos received an injury or injuries which were "non-survivable" without medical treatment.

Eventually, Fotis Dulos was charged with Murder, Felony Murder, and Kidnapping on top of earlier charges of Evidence Tampering and Hindering Prosecution. Also charged with Conspiracy to Commit Murder were Fotis's former girlfriend, Michelle C. Troconis, and his friend Kent Mawhinney.

In January 2020, Fotis Dulos was scheduled to appear for a hearing. When he didn't show up for court police went looking for him. They found him at his home where he had taken his life.

At the time of this writing, Michelle Troconis and Kent Mawhinney are both free on bond. Mawhinney has said he will testify for the state if the case goes to trial.

From the beginning of an investigation, police must be thinking about going to court!

When you try and prosecute a murder case without the victim's body, you must be able to prove several things. You must first be able to convince a jury the victim is actually dead. Next, you need to show they were murdered and did not die of natural causes. Finally, the proof must show the defendant is the person who caused the death beyond a reasonable doubt.

These cases are rare, but, somewhat surprisingly, they often result in a successful prosecution. Perhaps because everyone involved in the investigation and prosecution understands in order to obtain a guilty verdict they are going to have to bring their "A" game and perform a totally thorough investigation.

THE WRONG MAN? - NOT HARDLY!!

An article written by Cassandra Stephenson in the *Jackson Sun* (Jackson Tn. March 31, 2019) described efforts of the Innocence Project to examine the brutal murder of Donna Perry of Haywood County Tennessee in 1986. Jimmy Campbell was arrested for the crime. Following his arrest, Mr. Campbell confessed and eventually pleaded guilty to the murder. Ms. Stephenson did a good job of objective reporting especially considering there are limited court records or media accounts about the case. The only court proceedings involved were a suppression hearing in reference to the confession and the acceptance of Campbell's guilty plea. The killer was paroled in March 2018 after spending over 30 years in prison.

The article quotes Innocence Project staff attorney Bryce Benjet as saying, "This is the kind of case where certainly all of the risk factors for a wrongful confession are there." He goes on to discuss such things as mental disabilities, lengthy interrogation, and lack of other physical evidence. He says Campbell was first diagnosed with mental retardation in 1972 and had been a patient at Western Mental Health Institute 3 times. According to a court-ordered evaluation, Campbell had behavioral problems, struggled in school, had difficulty controlling his emotions, and experienced hallucinations.

While we would not disagree that a person with these personality characteristics might be prone to making a false confession, these same characteristics are exhibited by people who resort to violent behavior as a means of coping. Perhaps if a person with this type of personality was disappointed, frustrated, or felt rejected, he might respond with a violent outburst, such as stabbing someone 20 or 30 times and beating them to death.

According to the article, clinical psychologist John E. Sawyer wrote that Campbell might be unable to "withstand stressful situations". He might attempt to avoid and escape the stressful situation by fabricating any story that might "cause immediate reduction" of the stress.

It is not unusual for a person who has stabbed another human more than 20 times and then brutally beaten them until he was sure they were dead, to be a bit stressed when the police begin to ask questions about the murder. They can relieve the stress by telling the truth about what they have done and removing the guilt from their conscience.

There is also mention of the length of time Campbell was interviewed.

Our apologies to the people from the Innocence Project, but the length of time the interviewing process takes is totally dependent on how long it takes the person being interviewed to tell the truth. It would please the police if murderers would call, make an appointment for an interview and as soon as they are read their rights, tell the truth, the whole truth, and nothing but the truth. It just doesn't happen that way very often. In this particular case, it was never disputed that Mr. Campbell was given his rights to silence under the Miranda ruling every time he was questioned. The defendant confirmed this in open court several times when asked by Circuit Judge Dickie German. Campbell also stated he *understood* his rights to silence. In other words, by his own admission, he understood he could stop answering questions at any time. He also understood the would court appoint him an attorney any time he wanted one.

The Innocence Project comments on the lack of physical evidence. The police can only deal with the evidence they have. Evidence cannot be manufactured. In this case, all of the evidence that was discovered was tested and pointed to Mr. Campbell as the guilty party.

The Innocence Project is asking for DNA testing to be performed. There is a very small chance any evidence of value for DNA testing will be discovered. Thirty years ago no one had any idea DNA testing would be available in the future and the way evidence was packaged did not protect the integrity of the evidence for such an extended length of time. It is worth noting that the mere presence or absence of DNA evidence does not necessarily prove guilt or innocence. DNA, much like a fingerprint, is circumstantial evidence and most of the time an investigation is required to give meaning to circumstantial evidence.

There are also claims in the article that certain court rulings may have been unconstitutional. The Court of Criminal Appeals as well as the Tennessee Supreme Court upheld the conviction. Judge Clayburn Peeples denied a motion for DNA testing and the Innocence Project specifically questions the constitutionality of this ruling. Judge Peeples has taught Criminal Justice in college, served as an Assistant District Attorney, then as Attorney General, and currently is a Circuit Court Judge. It would an exercise in understatement to say Judge Peeples *is at least as knowledgeable* concerning constitutional law as the staff attorneys with the Innocence Project.

As mentioned earlier, the Innocence Project staff raised the possibility that Mr. Campbell made a false confession. While false confessions occur, they are very rare and there is no evidence in this case that the defendant's confession was anything but willful and truthful. He told certain things no one but the murderer could have known. Some would suggest he could have been given these facts (this is known as "leading" the suspect) in order to make his confession more credible. The investigators involved in this case were very professional and their integrity was of the highest level.

One of the officers who transported Campbell to court the day he entered his guilty commented that the killer was openly talking about committing the murder, almost in a joking fashion.

The Innocence Project does a great job and the people who work with the program have the best intentions.

In this particular case, Mr. Campbell confessed, pleaded guilty and the conviction was upheld through the appeals process. The case was investigated thoroughly and properly.

We know because we were there. Jimmy Campbell is guilty of this murder.

THE TRUTH, THE WHOLE TRUTH, AND NOTHING BUT THE TRUTH .... Really?

Two high profile murderers made "confessions" lately. Chris Watts very brutally murdered his pregnant wife and their two children. Watts pleaded guilty to 4 counts of first-degree murder and received consecutive life sentences for each one. Jake Patterson kidnapped an innocent young girl, after murdering her parents, and held her hostage for 3 months before she escaped. Jake says he will plead guilty at his next court hearing. Let's take a little more in depth look at what was said by these cowardly killers.

In the beginning, Watts tried to say his family disappeared. When the noose tightened, he changed his story and claimed he killed his wife, Shanann, because she killed the children. Watts now says he and his wife had a "discussion" and he admitted to having an affair. She threatened to divorce him and take the children. He says he felt like something had "snapped" inside of him because of the rage he was feeling. He strangled his wife to death. According to expert testimony, death by strangulation would probably have taken 2-4 minutes. Watts says his wife did not struggle. It is hard to imagine anyone being strangled to death and not putting forth some kind of resistance. In an effort to further distance himself from the evil of his act he said maybe she was praying and compared his murderous act with the crucifixion of Christ. Watts referred to Jesus asking The Father to forgive the people who were killing him and speculated Shanann may have been asking God to forgive her murderer while he was killing her. The killer says it was as if "other" hands were on top of his while he was choking the life out of his wife and those "other" hands wouldn't let him stop killing her. Watts went on to say it was like he had lost his mind and "didn't know what had happened."

While he was wrapping his wife's body up in a sheet in preparation for the disposal of her body, the children walked in. One of the children said, 'What have you done to Mommy?". Watts carried his wife's dead body about 45 minutes away to one of his worksites to bury her body. His two children, Celeste, 3, and Bella, 4, were with him riding in the back seat. Upon reaching his work site he strangled Celeste while she sat next to her sister. He forced her dead body into a petroleum pit and returned to his truck to kill Bella. Of course, the older daughter had seen everything that happened to her sister and had to know her father had killed her mother. She begged her father not to kill her. Watts says the last words his daughter spoke were "Daddy, NO!" The medical examiner found evidence she fought back, but of course, she was overpowered. This daughter was also stuffed into a petroleum vat. The monster used the same blanket to strangle both children and after killing them he buried his wife.

The killer says he reads the Bible every day now that he is in prison. Watts says he did not plan the murder, saying he asks himself the question, "did I know I was going to do that?" He goes on to say, "It just felt like there was already something... and I had no control over it."

Jake Patterson abducted Jayme Closs after he murdered her parents in cold blood at their home. Three months later Jayme escaped. When police questioned Patterson he said he targeted Jayme randomly when he saw her getting on a school bus. He later surveilled her home to ascertain the right time to make his murderous attack. He tried to impress the police with how smart he is by saying he cut his hair to keep from leaving DNA evidence. The murderer also bragged about hiding Jayme in the trunk of his car and driving past the police.

A reporter sent Patterson a letter asking him several questions and last week the killer responded.   He told a little different story. He told the reporter he did not plan the crime at all and he knew he would get caught. Patterson says he was surprised it took the police so long to catch him.

According to his latest rendition, the killer kept up with what the news reported about Jayme's disappearance and her parent's murder investigation by following social media. He says if it came on TV he would change the channel and didn't know what Jayme knew about what had happened or what was going on. He is trying to give the impression he was actually her *protector*.

When captured, the coward did not resist and immediately began telling his story. Patterson now claims police changed his statement to make him appear to be a cold, calculated killer. He also says he told police everything so they would not need to subject Jayme to an interview and further traumatize her. The murderer claims he will plead guilty as soon as possible so he won't put Jayme through any more anguish.

These two situations are classic examples of people who are guilty and want to confess, for one reason or another, but also want to minimize their guilt. They may want to justify their actions to the court to receive a better sentence, or try and relieve the burden of guilt on their own heart. In some instances, they may be concerned about the opinion of significant others concerning what happened. Below are some of the justifications offered by the killers.

1. *It really wasn't my fault.* According to Watts he and his wife were having a *discussion* and that *discussion* ended up with him confessing to having an affair. Perhaps the *discussion began* with questions about an affair?

Perhaps it wasn't the first time the couple had argued about his infidelity.   He goes on to say he became violent when his pregnant wife threatened to divorce him and take the children. Let's make sure we got this straight. Watts became violent and killed his wife because she was going to take their two lovely children away from him. This would be the same two precious children he murdered an hour later.

2. *I was forced to do it by factors outside of my control.* Watts seems to want us to believe the murders happened as uncontrollable incidents and were really outside of his control. Let's see, he choked her to death and strangulation is one of the most cold blooded and brutal ways to kill someone. He would have been face to face with his pregnant wife for

several minutes watching her die and she was probably begging for her life and the life of their unborn child. He says there was an *unknown pair of hands* on top of his hands. Watts would make us believe this paranormal pair of hands wouldn't allow him to stop choking his wife. The *Son of Sam* claimed a dog ordered him to kill people and now this guy has a mysterious pair of hands forcing him to murder his wife.

3. *It's all about me.*
In Watts' interviews with the media, he says his "house was incomplete" without his wife and children. He showed no remorse for the family he had just murdered. He was only concerned with how *he was affected*. It is unbelievable how a person could shop for sympathy after doing what he had done.

4. *I am not sure what happened.*
   When he was first arrested, it seemed as though Patterson wanted to brag about how smart he was and how well he planned the crime. He even said he cut his hair to try and avoid leaving DNA evidence at the crime scene. Now wants us to believe that nothing was planned and everything just *sort of happened.*
5. *Maybe I was a little bad, but they were worse!*
   Jake Patterson wants to direct the blame toward anyone besides himself. In responding to the reporter's questions he tried to blame the police for any trauma Jayme may experience. This is the "Maybe I was bad, but they were bad too." defense. I bet your mother wouldn't have fallen for the defense that someone did worse than you! She

probably would have told you that what the other kids had done did not matter to her!

6. *I didn't really do anything very bad.*
   Of course, the ultimate denial of guilt is the fact that Patterson doesn't address the parent's murders at all. The defense mechanism in his warped mind is trying to convince that if he doesn't talk about it, it will "go away".

After testifying in a first-degree murder case, the defendant's father approached me after testified to the confession the man's son had made. The father said, "I didn't believe Kenneth did it, but after hearing you testify, you should have tied him to the bumper of your car and drug him until he was dead." That would be too good for Watts and Patterson. They are true monsters.

SANTA FE HIGH SCHOOL MURDERS

The Murders

On May 18, 2018, on Friday at approximately 7:30 a.m., a seventeen-year-old male entered the Santa Fe High School in south Texas and opened fire with a shotgun and a .38 caliber revolver. The attack started just after classes began and the murderer used surprise to kill ten and wound twelve others. We will call the murderer "C.S."

The art classroom was the killer's main target and once he entered the room, he was heard yell "Surprise!". Then he started shooting. Since he was a student, the murderer was aware of the active shooter training the students received. He opened fire on the closet, knowing that would be one of the victim's hiding place. He killed 2 defenseless children hiding in the closet. Then he barricaded the room to keep police out and began searching other hiding places looking for more victims. The killer admitted he intended to kill the victims and didn't want to shoot people he liked because he wanted his story told.

C.S. was taken into custody by armed school resource officers stationed on the campus approximately 30 minutes after the attack began. He shot one officer and engaged another, then said, "If I come out, don't shoot me".

The Investigation

A student and a substitute teacher saw the killer shortly after the shooting began and they barricaded their classroom. The teacher pulled the fire alarm and students began to evacuate. A student said that at one point while they were evacuating, "like it was a fire drill". In another area, they began hearing gunfire and started running, even though teachers were telling them to stay where they were. Another student said after the gunfire, the teacher was telling them to run.

Responding to hearing a "bang" a teacher and student next door to the art room saw the killer run out, after firing 3 more shots, and they realized what was happening.

The Murderer

The murderer was wearing a trench coat to hide the weapons. Supposedly he had been wearing the coat and heavy boots frequently in the last few weeks.

A classmate described the killer, saying. "He was really quiet and he wore, like, a trench coat almost every day."

Police discovered writings on the killer's computer and cell phone.

All indications are he acted alone.

The Shooting

Explosive devices including pipe bombs and pressure cookers were found at the scene and near the school. None were functional. One pressure cooker was fitted with an alarm clock and projectiles (nails) but it did not contain any explosive material. There was also a Molotov cocktail, but it was never ignited. Police believe the IEDs may have been built in a nearby trailer.

C.S. documented his thoughts on computer and cell saying he intended to attack the school and then commit suicide. He tended to copy elements of the Columbine murders: black trench coat, shotgun, and explosives. More than 30 shooters have admitted to copying Columbine according to University of Alabama criminology professor Adam Lankford.

His social media accounts show several images of guns and a photograph of a long dark coat sporting Nazi symbols. His booking photo shows him wearing the "Born to Kill" T-shirt.

The killer's father says his son was a victim of bullying at school but school officials deny these allegations. It almost seems as though "bullying" has become an excuse for any kind of deviant behavior a person exhibits.

The mother of one of the victims said the C.S. had been trying to have a relationship with her daughter for about four months. When the victim rejected his advances, the killer became more and more aggressive until finally, she embarrassed him in front of other students about a week before the murders.

Police have not addressed the motive except to say the killer "wanted his story told".

According to reports, the murderer did not show any significant disturbing activity before the incident and he had no criminal record or official history of violence.

He Said...

The killer waived his right to silence and spoke with the police. He said he wanted to commit suicide after the murders, but didn't have the courage to kill himself. He said he purposely left some of the students he liked alive so they could tell the story of what happened. Those he didn't like were slaughtered.

The murderer said no one else was involved and police say they have seen no evidence anyone else participated in the act or the preparation.

In the Aftermath...

Parents fled to other schools to pick up their children.

Programs were put in place to help the school meet national guidelines for threat assessments.

If access control is enhanced at the school other considerations should be taken into account. We will not bring up these issues on social media and risk the chance of giving some coward ideas. Any school official or law enforcement officer who would like to review these concerns can contact us at *jleachtsg@msn.com*.

Some Changes Were Made

* School officials got 9 new metal detectors at entrances

* Installed bullet-resistant glass at the front vestibule

* Installed more security cameras hired more armed officers

* Placed panic buttons in every classroom.

    They also enhanced anti-bullying measures and began monitoring social media for possible warning signs. Programs were put in place to help the school meet national guidelines for threat assessments.

KEY ISSUES

> C.S. said he "wanted his story told". That is the only thing close to a motive we know. That is why he is referred to by initials. They are not his real initials.

> He told police he wanted to commit suicide but didn't have the courage. We can agree that he was not courageous, but the part about wanting the police to kill him seems to conflict with his statement when he surrendered. He is reported to have said, "If I come out, don't shoot me!"

> It should be noted the murderer was taken into custody by a School Resource Officer. After the tragedy, the school hired more armed officers. Experts disagree about whether the presence of armed officers is a good thing or not. The folks at Santa Fe High School *actually went through* the horrible experience of losing 10 lives in a school massacre and they decided to hire armed officers.

> C.S. brought improvised explosive devices (I.E.D.'s) to the school but they did not detonate.

> The murderer had no official record of violence or other criminal activity. The absence of an official record of violence does mean a person does not have violent tendencies or has committed violent acts. *It simply means no acts of violence have been reported properly and maintained in the system.* If a student is acting goofy, the other students will be the first to recognize the behavior. There must be an effective way for students to pass that information along to school officials!

> The student's description of confusion during the evacuation phase emphasizes the need to communicate and rehearse the crisis response plan. This particular event also illustrated a potential problem training may introduce into the situation. C.S. had been through the school's active shooter training so he knew the tactics that would be used by

staff and students as well as areas that were considered to be safe hiding places. Keeping this in mind, if school officials are made aware of a high-risk student that has left the school, certain parts of the training may need to be changed.

> It seems sort of strange that student assassins would still be attracted to Columbine, but they are! A kid wearing a long black trench coat needs to make the antennas go up!

THE ACCELERATOR WAS IMPRINTED ON HER SHOE

The young lady, let's call her Mary, was traveling east to west on Interstate 40 in Tennessee headed to the mountains of Arkansas. Records indicate she stopped at a rest area about 50 miles east of Jackson and used a payphone to call her husband in Arkansas. This was long before we had cell phones!

After placing the call, she got back on the Interstate and continued westbound. Mary stopped in Jackson Tn. and bought gas at a convenience store on North Highland Avenue. This chain of events seemed sort of strange. Why didn't she wait until she got to Jackson to call her husband instead of making an extra stop at the rest area? Maybe she needed to use the restroom and decided to call while she was there. You can think of several plausible reasons, I guess. Still, to a skeptical, young TBI agent, it seemed a little strange. Things would get a whole lot stranger.

Mary returned to the Interstate, traveled approximately 8 miles west of Jackson, and ran directly into a bridge abutment killing herself and her unborn child. She was 8 months pregnant.

There was a perfect imprint of the car's accelerator on the sole of her right shoe. Mary never touched the brake. Perhaps she fell asleep. But she had been awake enough to gas up her car only 10 minutes before she died. The evidence was enough for the District Attorney to ask for a TBI investigation.

It is normal in any kind of a death investigation to try and view the deceased's body, so I went straight to the funeral home when I was assigned the case. It was not long after her death, maybe 48 hours, but I really don't think it was quite that long. The husband, we'll call him Karl, had already had his wife cremated. No funeral, no memorial service, nothing. Cremation was not frequently done back then.

THP Sgt. Ben Joyner and I interviewed Karl at the Highway Patrol office in Jackson. We learned he was a retired scientist and at least 30 years older than his wife. He was a small man, dressed in black pants and a black shirt. He wore his white hair long and his similarly white beard reached the middle of his chest. He was very nice and soft-spoken but shared very little information.

Ben and I discussed it after the fellow left. Just talking to Karl and being in the same room with him gave us a funny feeling. It was weird.

About a week later I began getting mail from Mary's mother who lived in Florida. She shared a very unusual story with me and sent me a picture of her daughter. Mary was strikingly beautiful.

It seems Karl was the leader of some type of a religious cult based somewhere in the Ozarks. Mary's mother and father were members of the group.

Mary was enrolled in medical school at a college in Hawaii. During a school break, she came home to visit her parents. It just so happened Karl was visiting her parents at the same time. Shortly thereafter Mary dropped out of medical school, married Karl, and announced she was pregnant.

Attempts by her parents to intervene in this series of events were unsuccessful.

About 6 weeks after Mary's death I was contacted by Bill. Bill was an insurance investigator and he wanted to speak with me about Karl. We met in Jackson and had coffee.

It was common to see small, $10,000 life insurance policies for sale everywhere. You could buy them at just about any grocery store. The insurance investigator told me Karl had 10-15 of these types of policies on Mary. Bill explained having that a large number of small policies could indicate the beneficiary (Karl) was trying to keep from being noticed. Instead of having one $150,000 policy, you get 15, $10,000 policies, each from a different company. You hope, since the money is broken up into smaller amounts, the company will just pay it off and go on about their business.

It seems poor old Karl had some bad luck. Mary was the third wife who had died under mysterious circumstances. They all were insured by multiple small life insurance policies with Karl being the exclusive beneficiary on each one of the policies!

I never knew if Bill was able to put together any type of a fraud case or if the insurance companies refused to pay off the policies.

If, in fact, some criminal act had taken place in Mary's tragic death, we had no proof.

Obviously, Karl was a charismatic figure. Is it possible he had such control of Mary that he could convince her taking her own life was the right thing for her to do? Maybe there was some kind of hypnotic suggestion and he triggered her subconscious when she made the call from the rest area. If that were the case, why would she drive so far, stop, get out of her car, and gas up before driving into the bridge? Perhaps that was an effort to distance the act from the phone call. If you are planning on killing yourself, why gas up the car?

And what about a mother taking part in killing her unborn child? That is not unheard of, but it is VERY rare. When it happens it is usually because the pregnancy is the triggering event in ending an already troubled life. The expectant mother has no money, two other children already, no man to help, substance abuse problems. Things of that nature. The thought of bringing another child into this world and having the responsibility of rearing the child is simply more than the mother can handle. It happens. There was no evidence Mary suffered from any of these challenges.

Was this one of those cases where forces outside of our normal understanding come into play? Perhaps. May Mary rest in peace.

"WHAT ABOUT THE SKULL AND CROSSBONES?"

Mary was really a pretty nice lady. She had suffered a work-related accident and had drawn government subsidies ever since. The fixed income wasn't real great, so after a while, Mary decided she needed to create a little extra cash flow. Following an in-depth study of opportunities, Mary concluded the sale of untaxed liquor in a "dry" county could be an answer to her money problems. As Mary explained it, if you could afford to join the country club, you could drink all you wanted. She concluded she was only providing a service to those hard-working folks who couldn't afford to be members of the country club. The avoidance of paying sales taxes on liquor sales is not a big issue as far as bootleggers are concerned!

Joe moved in with Mary because he loved her. He was a good man. Joe had a decent job, had never been in any trouble, and everybody liked him. Almost everybody. Joe and Mary had a very nice relationship except for one small problem.

Roger lived just down the road. He was Mary's ex-boyfriend. He loved Mary too.

Roger happened to be a sure enough alcoholic. In a way, it was handy to live just down the road from his bootlegger. It was also a bit of a problem since Joe wasn't real crazy about Mary's old boyfriend hanging around the house.

The problem came to a head one afternoon when Roger needed a drink and he came to Mary's house to get one. As luck would have it, Mary was gone to Bolivar to shop. To make matters worse, she was out of liquor. When Joe told Roger there was no liquor to be had, Roger did not take it very well. That is putting it mildly.

Roger accused Joe of withholding the much needed liquor just because he was Mary's ex-boyfriend. Roger said Joe would not sell him anything to drink because Joe was jealous! Roger also threatened Joe with bodily harm if he did not sell him a bottle.

Remember, there was no liquor in the house. Mary was out!

After being chastised, berated, and threatened because he wouldn't sell Roger a half-pint, Joe decided to figure out something to do. He knew Roger was already drunk and probably wouldn't know the difference, so, Joe filled up a half-pint bottle (bootleggers usually have several around) and sold it to Roger.

Later that day the Sheriff's Department got a call from the hospital. There had been an unattended death that the hospital thought looked suspicious. It was Roger.

Sheriff Delphus Hicks and I were together working on something else that day. We began to investigate as soon as we got the call. Delphus was one of the best investigators I ever met.

After a few inquiries, we found out the last time anyone saw Roger, *alive*, was when he headed to Mary's house to buy a bottle.

Following up on that lead, we discovered Mary would not have been at home and Roger would have been dealing with Joe. It was pretty obvious this was a recipe for disaster!

We went to Mary's house and Joe was there.

Joe was cooperative. As a matter of fact, we stood out on the road in front of the house talking to Joe so long, the Sheriff's office got worried because we weren't answering the radio for such a long time. We didn't have cell phones or pagers or any of that. Dispatch had no idea where we were and, fearing the worst, everybody was looking for us!

Conducting a really good interview demands that you be willing to spend time with the person you are interviewing. We stood on the side of the road behind Sheriff Hick's car for at least 2 hours talking to Joe. At one point we knelt and prayed to ask the Lord to lead us to the truth about what happened to Roger.

Joe finally told us he poured something in a bottle and sold it to Roger. He just wanted Roger to leave him alone and go away. When we asked him what he poured in the bottle and sold to Roger, Joe said he wasn't sure.

Delphus asked if he could show us the bottle he poured from to fill up the half-pint bottle he sold to Roger. He showed us a bottle in the garbage. It was Singletary's Pest Control...

All three of us stood there at the garbage can for a moment. You could have heard a pin drop. Sometimes silence can be a very strong incentive to make a suspect speak. Delphus and I were both looking at Joe. We had built a good relationship after several hours of being together.

Finally, I said, "Joe, this is pest control. You knew that would kill Roger." Joe replied, "Man. I can't read. I didn't really know what it was."

Sheriff Hicks spoke up and said, "Mr. Smith, what did you think that skull and crossbones on the label meant?"

Joe couldn't answer that. He just hung his head. We arrested him for murder and carried him to jail.

The medical examiner's opinion was that if Roger hadn't been so hardcore, the poison wouldn't have killed him. He would have thrown up after a few swallows and it would have just burned his throat. His alcoholic condition made it possible for him to "kill" the whole half-pint. When he killed the half-pint, it killed him.

Joe pleaded guilty to a manslaughter charge. Nobody really thought he meant to kill Roger, it just happened.

When Joe entered his guilty plea he was allowed to go home to get his affairs in order and report to jail in a couple of weeks.

The prosecutors who handled the case gave him a ride home because he didn't have a car. Prosecutors giving a defendant a ride home may seem strange to some folks who think police and the people they have to arrest automatically hate one another. This is not necessarily true.

Chief Deputy George Bynum explained it to me perfectly when I was a brand new TBI Agent. He said, "Agent, we gotta go to war, but we gotta get along." He meant that people are going to make mistakes and the police must deal with the consequences of those mistakes. Once we deal with it, it's over, and if we treat them with respect, and they treat us with respect, we can all get along and live together.

My friend George passed away several years ago. I wish he could be here to explain that to everybody today.

"YOU STILL GOT THE BLOOD ON YOUR HANDS!"

What A Serial Killer Thinks

The case was 5 years old and about as cold as a case can be. We had run down every possible lead we could find.

I had gone so far as to meet with FBI Profiler Roy Hazlewood at the FBI National Academy in Quantico Virginia. It was 1983 and I was studying serial offenders as part of my training at The Academy. Roy was one of the original profilers in the Behavioral Science Unit and he was fantastic. I had never heard about serial killers before, but the more Roy talked, the more interested I became.

At my request, Mr. Hazlewood agreed to take a look at my cold case. I called the TBI office in Nashville and asked for a copy of the case file to be sent to me. They said the TBI file was confidential and they couldn't send it to me. I was a little bit upset. Of course, they didn't seem to be very concerned about whether I was upset or not. Ha!

Special Agent Hazelwood discussed the case with me for about an hour. He reminded me several times that any conclusions he reached would be "informal" since he had no case file and no autopsy report to review. At the end of our conversation, he said, "OK, here's what I think you are looking for." He gave me 8-10 characteristics the killer would possess. He and I both hoped, one day we would find out if Roy was on target with his thoughts. We would have to find the murderer to know for sure.

About a year after I graduated from The National Academy, the Jackson Tennessee Police Department got a call from the Madison County Alabama Sheriff's Department. A vehicle from Jackson was spotted at a suspected drug dealer's residence in Huntsville Alabama. Deputy Al Duffee from Alabama wanted a background check on the owner of the vehicle.

After discussing the information about the owner of the car (and yes, he was a drug dealer), the Alabama officer said, "By the way, we got a guy in jail for murder that used to live in Jackson."

Thank goodness the local officer taking the call was my old partner, Dennis Mays. He was one of the sharpest officers I ever knew and he immediately recognized the similarities between the murder in Alabama and our cold case.

Myself and an investigator from the police department traveled to Alabama to interview the suspect, Ken. He had been given a public defender since Ken could not afford to hire an attorney. We met with his attorney, and he asked, "Are you going to talk to him about his case in Alabama?" I replied, "With all due respect, we don't care what happened in Alabama, we are only interested in our murder in Tennessee." "If he'll talk to you, interview him all you want," the lawyer told us. We headed to the jail to talk to our suspect.

Ken was a big guy. He was unusually soft-spoken and polite. He had grown up in Jackson Tennessee and then hit the road. He traveled all over the country as an over-the-road truck driver and a carnival worker. He had no serious criminal history. After reading him his rights and telling him what we wanted to speak to him about, Ken readily agreed to talk to us.

We began by asking him about the different places he had lived and worked. Our questions centered around things we were familiar with and we asked questions we knew the answers to. This interviewing technique allowed us to observe what Ken's demeanor was when he was being truthful and when he was honestly trying to recall information to answer our questions. It is essential to know how a person looks and speaks when they are being honest if you are going to be able to detect when the person is being deceitful! This tactic is described as "getting a baseline" on the person you are interviewing.

During our conversation, Ken told us that he sometimes had issues with women. He told us about some problems with his former wife. He went on to describe how he would "pick up" girls in bars and attempt to have a relationship with them. He was becoming more emotional the longer he talked. He shared with us a scenario that sometimes developed when he was trying to "make out" with his victim.

By this time he was almost whispering and was staring at the floor. He appeared to have traveled to another world where only he could go.

While Ken was talking, I had slowly gotten out of my chair and eased around the desk. I pulled up another chair and began to move closer and closer to the suspect.

Ken continued recounting his experiences as if he was the only one in the room.

I was knee to knee with him when he whispered, "Sometimes when I'm making out with them, all of a sudden, they turn into my wife, and I hurt them, and I hurt them bad, and I don't care how bad I hurt them. Then I throw them out of the car. But I never killed nobody."

He was leaning over with his elbows resting on his knees. He was wrenching his hands so hard the muscles were standing out on his forearms. Tears were streaming down his face and his nose was running uncontrollably.

I began speaking to Ken.

It was the first time I had said a word since he had gone into "his world". I had my hand on his shoulder and I was talking very softly. "I know you didn't mean to kill them, Ken, you are not that kind of man." "I didn't kill nobody" he replied. "Ken, you have got to get this off your chest, it will kill you if you don't". I kept repeating that theme over and over again and in a minute Ken began to nod in agreement with me.

Ken and I had become companions. I was his friend, I understood. I was the guy he could tell a secret to.

The investigator with me decided this was the time he needed to get involved. He stood, put his hands on the desk, leaned over, and said, "Yeah, but you still got the blood on your hands".

Ken immediately straightened up and asked to go back to his cell.

There was almost another killing in Alabama that day...

It took me 5 trips to Alabama, but Ken finally confessed to the brutal murder. He was tried, convicted, and died on death row of natural causes.

Investigator Notes:

If more than one person is involved in an interview, pay attention to who the suspect is "connecting with" best. Let that person lead the interview. If you are the OTHER interviewer, SHUT UP!

Don't feel jealous because the suspect is exhibiting a better rapport with your partner. In the next interview, the suspect may relate to you best.

When the time is right, the primary interviewer should ask her partner for questions, and continue the interview from that point!

THE DISAPPEARING BULLET!

A family member found Betty lying face down on the floor of the modest trailer she called home. Betty lived there alone and was known in the small town she lived in as a good, hard-working woman.

She died from multiple gunshot wounds.

The murder occurred in the earl1980's in rural Hardeman County Tennessee near the Mississippi state line in Grand Junction. These were tough times in tough territory. A weekend of hard drinking after a week of hard work too often ended up in tragedy. Life was cheap.

I was a Special Agent for the Tennessee Bureau of Investigation at the time and my primary counties of responsibility were Hardeman and Fayette counties. The Sheriffs in both counties were kind enough to give me an office which I shared with the department's criminal investigators.

Each department probably had about 8 - 10 deputies. Bolivar and Somerville, the largest cities in each county, had a small police department with one officer in each department assigned as an investigator. None of us got paid overtime, so we all worked long hours. There was a lot of work to be done and very few officers to do it.

Such things as S.W.A.T. Teams and Crime Scene Units existed only in big cities like Memphis and on TV.

When you are conducting a criminal investigation, it is important to try and anticipate any questions defense attorneys may ask during a court proceeding. It is part of their job to uncover mistakes made during the investigation and they are very good at it!

Once when I was testifying in a murder case a good defense attorney drilled me because I had neglected to do my job thoroughly. We were having a preliminary hearing on a suspect we had arrested for murder. A large part of our proof rested on the information we received from an informant and during my time on the witness stand I was asked a question about the informant's criminal record. I responded (like a nitwit) that I hadn't had time to run a record check on the informant.

When he asked the question, the attorney was striding in front of the witness box. I answered, and he stopped in mid-stride and turned to face me. I had a bad feeling. The lawyer began by reminding me the organization I worked for, the TBI, was the repository for all the criminal records in the state. He then had me describe exactly how hard it would have been and how long it would have taken for me to run a record check. I, sheepishly, admitted all it would have taken was a phone call.

The lawyer then proceeded to "light me up" on the witness stand. He questioned why I had plenty of time to get a warrant and arrest his client for murder, but I didn't have the time to make a phone call to check the informant's record. Let me make it clear, I knew the informant was a convicted felon, but I had not requested his complete criminal history. I never made that particular mistake again.

Believe me, a good defense attorney can teach you a lot about being a good investigator!

In the case of Betty's murder, one of the issues we were trying to resolve was where all the bullets that had been fired in the trailer came to rest. This could be important for several different reasons. The location of the fired bullets might give us some indication as to whether the victim had been surprised by someone she didn't know, such as a burglar, or was confronted by someone she felt comfortable enough with to allow them to come into her home and get close to her. Of course, the bullets might also provide important ballistic evidence.

After reviewing the autopsy and speaking with the medical examiner it was apparent there was one bullet unaccounted for. That bullet could have been the last shot fired and maybe show the method of operation and motive, perhaps leading to a suspect.

Chief Cecil "Red" Wilson with the Grand Junction Police Department and myself returned to the crime scene, Betty's trailer, once again to try and find the missing spent round. We looked very carefully throughout the entire trailer, but we could not find a bullet hole.

We were just about to declare it a mystery bullet when Red had an idea. As was stated earlier, Betty was found lying face down on the floor. After looking at the autopsy, it was evident the bullet we were looking for traveled straight through her skull from the back of her head. There was a large blood spot on the carpet where her body was found. The carpet was some kind of indoor/outdoor material, sort of like astroturf. But there was no hole in the carpet that we could see.

Red and I stood around scratching our heads for a minute, trying to figure what had happened. Then without saying a word, Red reached down and grabbed a corner of the carpet and pulled it back. This move exposed the trailer floor and sure enough, there was a hole in the floor that looked like a bullet hole!

We still didn't have the bullet. Once again, without saying anything, Red walked into the bedroom and came out with a coat hanger. He straightened the coat hanger and ran it through the hole until it hit something solid. Since I had been absolutely no help to Red up to this point, I volunteered to crawl underneath the trailer and see what the coat hanger was hitting. It turned out to be the underpinning for the trailer.

It was dark underneath the trailer and I couldn't see very well. To be honest, I was a little preoccupied looking for snakes, too. When I reached up and felt the coat hanger, I just ran my hand all the way down the hanger until I hit the cross tie. My hand landed on the bullet.

After being shot several times, Betty apparently fell to the floor and at that point, her killer shot her in the back of the head. It looked like an execution.

After locating that final bullet it indicated to us the killer knew the victim and there was very probably a very personal motive. We quickly developed a prime suspect (the victim's boyfriend) and Sheriff Delphus Hicks and I spent several hours talking to him on more than one occasion. At one point we took a lengthy written statement from him. The statement was 11 handwritten, legal-size pages long. It was full of lies.

The next day we met with District Attorney General Paul G. Summers. He would be given the task of prosecuting the case if we made an arrest. Paul said Sheriff Hicks and I had done a good job of proving the suspect was a *liar*.

*But his statement did not prove he was a **murderer**.*

It is important to remember to convict a person of a crime you must *prove they committed every element of that particular crime!* General Summers taught me a valuable lesson that day.

Having said that. It is still important to listen to a suspect's lie and document them. A good liar will try and stay as close to the truth as possible and the lie mat give you some good leads to follow up on. The lie may also tip you off as to what the suspect's alibi is going to be. Finally, if the suspected killer takes the witness stand, his statement may be used to cross-examine him and ruin his credibility if he tries to lie while under testifying oath.

I don't remember if Chief Wilson had much formal police training in crime scene investigation or not, and I don't care. No matter what kind of investigative aids science produces, common sense and good investigative technique will always be important.

This incident is just one more example of how valuable good old basic police work can be.

THE PARKLAND HIGH SCHOOL MASSACRE

The Murders

The killer, who we will call H.C., arrived at Marjorie Stoneman Douglas High School in Parkland Florida in an Uber at 2:19 PM on February 14, 2018. By the time he was finished, a total of 17 students and staff members had been murdered.

An unlocked gate gave him access to building 12 where the murders occurred. The gate was unlocked 20 minutes before the time for student dismissal. School officials said the gate wasn't manned because of a lack of personnel. The teacher who was unlocking the gates recognized H.C. as a former student who some people referred to as "Crazy Boy". They also recalled several faculty and staff predicted H.C. was the student most likely to "shoot up the school". The murderer was carrying a rifle bag when he entered through the gate.

H.C. warned a student friend to leave the school and the student reported this warning to one of the school's coaches. The student also told the coach he had seen H.C. loading a rifle. One teacher saw H.C. with the rifle inside Building 12 and did nothing. The same teacher later heard shots fired and ducked into a janitor's office. No one called a "Code Red" until 3 minutes and 16 seconds after the first shot had been fired.

An after-action report found there were no definite criteria for when to declare a *Code Red* or who was responsible for deciding to call for a *Code Red* response. The report went on to say there was "no policy, little training, and no drilling (practice)" about declaring or reacting to a Code Red. The report concludes these factors left everyone more vulnerable to an active shooter situation.

The killer only shot people within his line of sight and he never actually entered a classroom. There were no coverings for the windows, so H.C. was able to see inside the classrooms from the hallway. Some victims were in classrooms with no *hard corners* and they could not hide from view. The killer's fired bullets went through drywall and metal doors and if he had realized this could happen, the incident probably would have been much worse.

H.C. wanted to become a *sniper* by setting up in a teacher's lounge on the third floor, however, the lounge was equipped with storm-resistant glass that wouldn't allow a decent viewing/firing situation.

Listed below are several factors that hindered the response to the mass murders.

1. The public address system did not work in the hallways or on the exterior

so it was inadequate in providing information.

2. The fire alarm sounded, maybe because of the smoke from the killer's weapon, and some students and staff responded by following evacuation procedures rather than sheltering in place. The attempts to evacuate may have put everyone at greater risk.

3. School policy did not allow viewing the video system in *real time*. This policy resulted in a twenty minute delay and was one reason officers were not aware Cruz had left building 12. The responding officers were under the impression the video was real time. What they thought was happening at the time they were seeing it on the video had actually happened 20 minutes before that time.

4. The 911 system did not disseminate information to the responding first responders in an efficient manner.

5. Radio communication suffered from a lack of interoperability and this affected tactical operations inside Building 12.

6. There was confusion about the location of the command post, the tactical operations center, and staging areas immediately after the murders. Law enforcement and fire department command posts were separate which caused a lag in communication.

The Investigation

The report produced by a state commission assigned to investigate the murders praised many officers for responding properly and rendering aid to the wounded and getting possible victims to safety. Most of the praise went to the officers from the Coral Springs Police Department. They attended training annually and responded as they had been trained.

* Some of the deputies were quoted as saying they could not remember the last time they had active shooter training and could not recall what type of training they had received. Many officers said additional training would have helped but also said no amount of training could have prepared them to face such an event.

* Officers did not immediately confront the shooter. Many of them failed to go toward the gunfire and thus failed to contain or neutralize the murderer.

* The report also criticizes officers for taking time to put on bullet-resistant vests and "gear up" before going into the building where shots were being fired. It should be noted that officers may not routinely be "geared up" to respond to a situation of this nature and if they responded without being properly equipped, they could have been more of a liability than an asset.

*Some officers arrived near the scene but stayed a distance away while shots were being fired rather than attempting to defuse the situation.

* The SRO was found derelict in his duty.

* Apparently there were repeated concerns expressed to school officials and law enforcement. At least 30 people knew of his *Troubling Behavior*".

* Surveillance cameras functioned inadequately due to the fact they did not cover the area as well as they should have and personnel were not well trained on the use of the camera system

* The report referred to the school as a "soft target".

In response to the report's criticisms, school officials said they planned to improve security policies and procedures, training, communications, physical hardening, and threat assessment.

His Behavior

Either they didn't report what they knew, or, they did report and nothing happened. Two students reported strange behavior but it was disregarded by school administrators. According to reports, H.C. said he liked to see people in pain, he looked up firearms on a school computer and also posted photos of firearms.

He once killed a duck with a tire iron, he shot squirrels with a pellet gun and decapitated a bird according to students, neighbors, and mother's co-worker's statements. He showed a student a photo of a decapitated cat he supposedly killed. One student said the murderer brought a knife and some bullets to school.

H.C. repeatedly made racial and anti-gay remarks and drew swastikas. He bragged on the murderer at the Pulse nightclub in Orlando.

He took time to research and make plans for his cowardly attack. He researched shooting guns and other attacks and studied the schedule at Parkland. He worked as a cashier to raise the money and also used money he inherited from his mother He displayed guns and threatened to kill his mother.

His mother said she was scared of him and told a friend if anything happened to her, "Nik did it".

There was no evidence H.C.'s actions met the criteria for him to be involuntarily examined under the rules of the *Baker Act* which would have prevented him from buying or possessing a firearm.

H.C. made at least 3 videos of himself – that's how many police recovered - expressing his feelings of loneliness and worthlessness. He also said on the videos he wanted to be remembered along with other mass murderers. He said this 4 times in just over 2 minutes of video. In one video he bragged, "When you see me on the news, you'll all know who I am. You're all going to die." He mimicked the video sound of gunfire.

The first video was February 8, the second was on February 11, and the last one was apparently on February 14th. He announced, "Today is the day". These were on his cell. While he was making the videos he was laughing and really enjoying himself. He bragged about what he was going to do and also talked about loneliness and feelings of worthlessness. "All the kids in school will run and hide, from the wrath of my power, they will know who I am", he bragged. "He continued, "I am going to be the next school shooter of 2018. My goal is at least 20 people." He described the weapons he planned to use and gloated, "I think I can do a good job."

In the second video, he goes into more detail but talks about shooting as many people as possible in the main courtyard. This didn't happen, but perhaps he planned to do this from the library window.

In one video he reflected on his life, saying he lived in "seclusion and solitude". "I am nothing. I am no one, my life is nothing and meaningless. With the power of the A.R. (his rifle), you will know who I am. A detailed tip to the FBI got no action

The killer went on to say he'd had enough of being told what to do, and being called "an idiot".

After the Murders

As H.C. was escaping, he dropped the AR-15 assault rifle he had used. In all the confusion none of the other students even noticed. They were too busy trying to save their lives by getting away from building 12. He didn't resist arrest an hour later when police caught him walking down the street.

The killer told police he spent about $4,000 on the small arsenal he had accumulated. During his questioning, H.C. said he had bought the weapons, including the AR-15 he used that day. He also said he bought 3 shotguns, and an AK-47 (another assault weapon) along with a lot of ammunition. The shooter left 180 rounds of ammunition when he fled the school. In a post on YouTube, the murderer announced he wanted to be a "professional school shooter".

It was a pattern H.C. would repeat throughout his questioning saying he was worthless, wanting to die, and wondering out loud why he wasn't killed.

He also said he didn't want to live and mumbled, "kill me". The statement was captured by a recorder while he was by himself. It appeared obvious he was playing to the camera, which he knew was monitoring him. The detective questioning him had stepped out to get the murderer a glass of water even though H.C. said he didn't deserve a glass of water.

H.C. told police he attempted suicide by taking Advil on one occasion and drinking vodka and tequila another time. He simply threw up and passed out. On the morning of the murders, he claimed he took a blunt knife and tried to hurt himself.

H.C. referred to himself as being "stupid" and a "coward".

He told police of a plan to go to a park and shoot people a few weeks before the murders at Parkland, but he backed out.

When questioned by police H.C. said he heard a "demon" voice inside his head telling him to "burn, kill, destroy". He continued by saying the voice also instructed him to take the Uber to Parkland School. He described the voice as a friend, "Because I have no one". He asked for a psychologist "to find out what's wrong with me". Records show he had seen mental health specialists for years, but when investigators asked about these consultations, he said he was afraid to tell the psychologists about the voice. H.C. said the voice calmed down when he took Xanax, smoked marijuana, or got some exercise.

When detectives began to indicate they had doubts about the existence of the voice, the coward asked for a lawyer and ended the interview.

When his brother was allowed to see C., he asked a very direct question. "What do you think mother would do if she could see you right now?". The coward answered, "She would cry."

KEY ISSUES

> The killer gained access to the school by entering through a gate that was unlocked 20 minutes before the student's dismissal. Apparently it was routine to unlock the gate every day at this time. The teacher noticed the murderer was carrying a rifle bag.

> There was confusion about when to declare a "Code Red" situation. A student reported to one of the coaches that H.C. warned him to leave the school and was loading a rifle. Another teacher saw H.C. inside Building 12 with the rifle.

> Several logistical problems hindered an effective response. The public address system did not function properly, the video was not running in "real-time", radio communications between first responders was poor, and

the 911 system did not route calls properly.

> The Sheriff's Department was criticized for its response. The lack of adequate training was blamed for its ineffective response. A school resource officer was charged criminally for his lack of response.

> At least 30 people were aware of the "troubling behavior" the murderer was exhibiting. This information was not analyzed properly. The killer was referred to as "Crazy Boy" and several school employees said he was the student "most likely to shoot up the school.

GOOD SHOOT... OR NOT?

When police must investigate an officer-involved shooting, many times you will hear them refer to the action as a "good shoot" or a "bad shoot". What this means is, was the officer justified in using, or attempting to use deadly force.

Please keep in mind police have the authority to use deadly force if deadly force must be used to save a life. In other words, a police officer can use deadly force to keep the person from killing themself (the officer), or someone else.

Police are taught to shoot to kill, not to shoot to disable. Remember, the only reason they can legally shoot is to neutralize a threat and save a life. If an officer were to try and shoot a knee or a hand, or some other part of the body in an attempt to disable a potential killer, what happens when the officer misses? That "miss" could allow the bad actor to continue with their plans and kill someone. Also, if the bullet misses the target, it might hit an innocent bystander.

Police frequently get criticized if multiple rounds are fired when attempting to contain a threat. There are countless examples of people who have been shot multiple times and continued to fight, shoot, and attack. It would be nice if there was a book that said, "OK, in this situation, you shoot twice, but if this happens, you can shoot five times.." Unfortunately, no such book exists. If the decision has been made that lethal force is required to eliminate a threat and that lethal force is gunfire, you shoot until the threat is neutralized.

We are not talking about target practice. Things are happening incredibly fast. Many times there has been a fight before employing deadly force. If you are an officer, EVERY FIGHT can turn into a fight for your life. If the threatening individual gets control of your weapon, you are most likely dead. Attempting to shoot when you are struggling for breath and adrenaline is pumping out the top of your head is not a recipe for precision fire.

Officers are taught to shoot center mass. If you shoot for center mass, even if you miss, you may hit some part of the body that will neutralize the suspect and save someone's life. Maybe your own.

There is a perception shooting someone in the back makes a "bad shoot". This is not true. In certain situations, such things as trajectory, angles, timing, etc.. may come into play during an investigation. No single factor, independent of all other evidence, decides the legality of a deadly force encounter.

No single factor determines whether or not it was a justified response. Good investigators put all the evidence together and then present it to a prosecutor for a decision.

Once the decision is made that lethal force is required, the officer's job is to stop the threat. Period.

The law does not say the officer had to utilize the BEST POSSIBLE solution to neutralize the threat. The law says the officer had to abide by the law in carrying out his duty. The justice system may take years to decide if the officer acted appropriately. The officer, who was under incredible stress, had a split second to decide what to do. It's a pretty tough job.

We recently published a podcast on Tennessee Underground Facebook page as well as TUGNEWS.COM reporting on the shooting of Jacob Blake by police in Kenosha Wisconsin and this blog is largely in response to the reaction by our friends to that podcast.

Please review this summary of what has been reported as the events that led up to the shooting of Mr. Blake.

The police were called and asked to respond to a domestic disturbance. A domestic disturbance is widely recognized as one of the most dangerous calls an officer must deal with. The people involved in a domestic disturbance are normally very emotional and there is a good chance weapons are within reach. It is not unusual for all parties involved to unite and see the police as the enemy.

The shooting occurred at about 5 p.m. on August 23, 2020. Investigators say the call was placed by a woman who said her boyfriend was present and he wasn't supposed to be on the premises. The Kenosha Police Association says the caller complained Blake was trying to steal her keys and car. It is very possible the caller said both things.

The responding officers are advised of outstanding felony charges against Mr. Blake. The charges included 3rd Degree Sexual Assault, Disorderly Conduct, and Criminal Trespass. All of these were classified as domestic abuse. Of course, the normal course of business would be to place him under arrest.

Mr. Blake resisted arrest and even continued to resist after being Tased. He was a member of the wrestling team at his high school. He probably had great physical skills to resist. Some accounts say he put one officer in a headlock.

Police pursued him, catching up to him as he tried to enter the vehicle. Three innocent children were in the vehicle Mr. Blake was attempting to use to elude arrest for a crime of violence. If he was planning on using the car to escape, he was risking the children's safety by involving them in a police pursuit event.

Reports say Blake told officers he had a knife. There are differing opinions as to whether or not the video shows a knife in Blake's hand. A knife was recovered by police in the driver's side floorboard of the vehicle. It is not clear at this point if the vehicle belonged to Blake or someone else.

Media spokespersons have emphasized the fact the shooting

occurred in front of the children. It should be noted, the police did not introduce the children into this situation, Mr. Blake did. He led the police to the car in his attempt to escape arrest.

Once he brought the fight to the car, the police had a responsibility to protect the children.

Let's see. This is what the officers knew.

Jacob Blake had a deadly weapon and a history of violence. He caused enough of a disturbance the police were called and he struggled with the officers. Their attempts to keep him from getting in the car, including trying to pull him back, failed. As a last resort, they shot him.

Some say Blake should have been allowed to drive away, with the children and the knife, and get arrested sometime in the future.

What happens when the children are hurt or killed in a crash when he is trying to get away from the police? Or

*they find the car 2 hours later with
three dead children inside?*

*Didn't those children deserve to be
protected from a violent man with a
knife?*

*Please don't argue the children
would have been safe with him because
he is their father. Fathers harm their
children far too often.*

It is important to understand police
MUST react to the situation as they
experience it. They act according to
what they see and hear while the event
is occurring.

Any knowledge of the history of the
people involved is probably limited to a
basic database record check. The
officer does not have the luxury of
hindsight

"IT WAS JIMMY B."

Many years ago when I was a TBI agent our agency was called to assist in the investigation of a terribly vicious murder in a county in western Tennessee. Several of us went to that county to help.

After a few days of running down leads, we were at a standstill. We were about out of leads and didn't have any solid suspects. This is not unusual when working on a mystery murder but it is VERY frustrating.

Back then we did not get paid overtime, but we had a murder to solve so it was not unusual for us to work around the clock to try and find the killer.

When I say "us", I do not mean just TBI agents. Out in "the country" there weren't that many officers, and when there was a bad murder, rape, kidnapping, or other such crime, we all worked together. County sheriffs, city police officers, and state officers all worked as long as possible with no thought of the clock.

Myself and TBI Agent Tommy Lewis were sitting at the jail when a lady came in and wanted to speak to an investigator involved in the murder investigation. She was brought to us and we interviewed her.

The lady told us she was the victim's aunt and she had dreamed about the murder. We asked her to tell us all about the dream. What the heck, we had nothing to lose!

In her dream, she saw a man chasing her niece through a field and the man had a large knife. The victim had been stabbed multiple times. We asked the obvious question. "Who was the man?. She replied she could not see his face. We asked her to come back and see us if she had a similar dream and could see his face. She promised she would do that. We just shook our heads and went back to work.

About two days later we were out in the car looking for somebody we needed to interview when we got a call to return to the jail. There was a woman there who wanted to talk to us. It was the aunt.

She said she had the dream again and this time she saw the man's face. We asked if she knew him and she said yes, it was Jimmy B. Tommy and I looked at our list of people who might possibly know something about the case, and way down at the bottom of the list, there was Jimmy B. We were going to interview him anyway, but, frankly, we were in no hurry. The only reason his name was on our list was someone told one of the investigators that Jimmy B. knew the victim. In any criminal investigation, but especially in one of this nature, you must be as thorough as possible, so even if it is as minor as someone saying you knew the victim, that will get your name on the list!

Later that morning one of the deputies called us and said there was a guy he was in contact with that we might want to interview. The deputy, who was a very sharp officer, had been in General Sessions court that morning when one of the prisoners walked up to him. The man, who the deputy did not know, said, "I just wanted to tell you, I didn't have nothing to do with killing that girl down there in the bottom." Please understand, no one had asked him about "killing that girl down there in the bottom".

He was in court to answer to the charge of driving while under the influence of an intoxicant. He was known to have a heavy beard and long hair. At some point after the murder he shaved the beard off and when we met him he was bald-headed. It was Jimmy B.

Jimmy B. confessed to the murder and eventually pleaded guilty to avoid the electric chair.

We never talked to the aunt again. Looking back on the case, I kind of wish I had gone back to talk with her a little more. Of course, we couldn't use her dream as evidence, so there was really no reason for us to bother her anymore. After all, she had already lost her niece and we certainly didn't want to add to her grief by bringing up the memory of the murder again.

Now and then in the police business (and in life), things happen that you just can't explain. Things that are outside the realm of our normal understanding. I certainly remember this incident as being one of those "things".

I will tell you this. After that experience, if someone tells me they had a dream about something, saw something that others couldn't see, or had a premonition, I take it very seriously.

Just because something happens that is outside our realm of understanding does not mean it didn't happen.

"IT'S JUST A LITTLE CUT..."

It was an especially violent murder scene. There was blood everywhere.

The evidence indicated there had been a fight in the bedroom and the victim lost. She was found lying on the floor, next to her bed. She had been stabbed multiple times and the autopsy confirmed stabbing to be the cause of death.

You could track the killer's path from the bedroom, through the kitchen, and into the bathroom by the trail of blood. There was blood all over the bathroom sink, as well as the floor and the tub. It looked like the murderer had been wounded and tried to stop the bleeding. There was a whole lot of blood in that bathroom.

Hospitals in a four-county area were checked to see if someone had shown up with a knife wound. The results were negative.

We asked for assistance from the Tennessee Bureau of Investigation Crime Lab in Donelson and they immediately sent a team of forensic specialists. These folks were true experts in working a crime scene. They photographed and drew sketches of the scene. Blood samples and trace evidence were collected. DNA was not a part of the game back then, but we could hope for blood type and maybe a sub-type. Fingerprints were developed and "lifted".

After several hours of tedious work, the crime scene technicians finished and headed back to the Crime Lab to analyze what they had found. Blood tests confirmed two separate blood types had been recovered from the scene, so our theory the killer had been wounded in the fight appeared to be correct.

Five TBI agents (including myself) were assisting the local police department in the investigation. It was a small department and virtually every officer was working on the case in some fashion. The sheriff's department helped with interviews and locating witnesses. As is usually the case in a vicious crime like this, everybody pitches in and works together. Many times there are problems between departments for various reasons, but at a time such as this, differences are forgotten for a while.

Our investigation revealed the victim to be a Dilaudid dealer. This was in the mid-1980s and Dilaudid was probably the most potent drug readily available in our rural area. Dilaudid was highly addictive and cost $50 a pill on the street. In short, people would kill you over Dilaudid.

You might as well have thrown the clocks away and had us leave our watches in the trunk of the car. We worked at least 48 hours without a break and sleep time was sparse for many days (and nights) following the initial investigative crush. We interviewed, photographed, and fingerprinted over 60 people in three days. Among other things, we were trying to find the last person or people to have seen the victim alive. We were assuming the motive was drugs or money or a combination of the two.

Of course, we were also looking for someone who had been wounded. Both men and women were thoroughly inspected for a knife wound. Male officers searched men and female officers searched the women. We found nothing.

Our investigation indicated there had been a party at the victim's home the night of her death. At least eight people were present at the party. The investigative theory was that the murderer was a member of the party group. If the killer was *not* the last person to leave the house, and someone else was still there when the fight broke out, then maybe we would be lucky enough to have a witness. Another hypothesis was that after the party broke up and everyone left, a Dilaudid customer showed up at the house, and, for whatever reason (probably a disagreement about money or dope) an altercation ensued and resulted in murder.

We worked with the assumption everyone at the party was a drug user. Before we ever asked them the first question, we assured them we were not interested in drugs right now. We were working on a homicide.

The people who attended the party admitted to being there and admitted drugs were involved. When it came to anything more than those admissions, nobody knew nothing about nothing.

The folks from the lab were staying in close contact with us and one day when I was speaking with one of the fingerprint experts (Bob), I mentioned the fact we hadn't found anyone with a cut. Bob immediately said, "What about Mike ?" Mike was one of the partygoers the night of the murder. I told Bob we had interviewed Mike more than once, and since he was there that night he was considered a possible suspect. I followed up by noting that Mike wasn't cut. Bob interrupted me. 'I was just looking at his fingerprint card and he had a cut on his left index finger when he was printed". Bob faxed me a copy of the fingerprint card and sure enough, you could see a very small cut. It looked like a "paper cut".

I thanked Bob for all his help. I was thinking to myself, "A cut on his finger?? That type of wound wouldn't produce enough blood for what we saw at the scene. That bathroom looked like somebody had been killing hogs in there!"

A few days later the Chief of Police called. He had just talked with someone who knew Mike and she informed the Chief that Mike and his wife were going to California the next day. I asked the Chief if he could round them up so we could question them again.

He found them and we interviewed the two of them for quite some time. Once again they admitted to being at the party and using drugs. They denied any knowledge of the murder.

Oh yeah, the cut on Mike's finger had healed. I questioned him about having a cut on his finger the first time we interviewed him. He said he didn't have a cut on his finger and didn't know what I was talking about.

Uh-Oh...

Of course, when he lied about the cut it made him look more guilty. Why would he lie about the cut on his finger if it didn't mean anything?

When interviewing a suspect you try and develop a **theme.** Generally speaking, themes come in all shapes and sizes. The interviewer can appear to be empathetic or hard-nosed, agreeable or disgusted, non-accusatory, or convinced of guilt. The trick is to pick out the theme that will work with this particular suspect at this particular time!

Whatever theme you decide to begin with, be prepared to change to another theme if the one you are using is not working. A good investigator must be ready, willing, and able to change their method of questioning and try to find the approach that will work!

In this interview we tried just about everything we could think of and nothing was working.

We decided to try a direct bluff. Yep, a big lie! The pair were told we were tired of playing games and we knew exactly what happened. We postulated that as the party was winding down, they left the victim's home, only to return a short time later shopping for more dope.

Problem was, they didn't have any money! What began as an argument started that ended up as a murder.

Investigators repeated the same theory over and over again along with pleas to tell the truth and at least show a little remorse. No deal. Nothing. We finally called it a night. They headed to California. Without a confession, we did not have enough evidence to charge either one of them.

Shortly after that, I moved to Nashville. Several months later Mike returned to Tennessee and one of my partners, TBI Agent Dennis Mays, questioned Mike again and this time he confessed to being the killer.

It turned out our theory was close to being right, but not exactly perfect!

Mike and his girlfriend never left, they just stayed until the other folks went home. We were right about the motive. Mike wanted to buy some Dilaudid on credit (It's called "fronting") and the dealer would not go along with it. The fight started and ended terribly.

The problem with making a direct bluff as we did is, if you aren't exactly right, the suspect knows you are lying. If an investigator gets caught bluffing, the odds are very slim the suspect is going to confess to that investigator.

Many times the question is raised as to how you explain bluffing in court. You tell the judge exactly what you said and did to try and sell the bluff. It is not against the law to bluff unless you threaten, coerce, make promises of leniency, or do any of the other things that are prohibited in interviewing a suspect.

YOUR BODY SPEAKS, BUT WHAT'S IT SAYING ?

A developing case that's in the news these days illustrates some important aspects regarding understanding body language.

Heide Broussard and her infant child disappeared on December 12, 2019, from Austin Texas. At the time of this writing, one of Heidi's best friends, Magen Fieramusca, is charged with kidnapping the baby and murdering Heidi. The baby is safe.

When Shane Carey, Heidi's fiance and the father of the child was giving a press interview asking for help finding his infant child and the child's mother, he exhibited certain body language gestures some considered strange. While making his pleas he covered his right eye with the back of his balled up his right fist and he consistently looked away from the cameras and interviewers. Were these gestures signs of guilt, or at the least, deceit?

Body language movements are classified into two broad groups. Open and closed. An open body language posture says you like the message you are receiving from the other person and you want to hear more! On the other hand, when we are getting a message that we perceive as threatening, our body "closes up" in an attempt to protect us from this perceived threat. Our automatic gestures create a demeanor that says, "I am feeling stress about this deal".

In our minds, if we no longer *see a threat, then the threat no longer exists.* To get some relief, we may put our hands in front of our eyes, increase the rapidity of our blinking, or, simply look away. These actions can take away the image of the threat in our minds and give us a little break from the stress!

OK, now we understand the guy has some kind of stress going on, so the next question, what is causing the stress?

In this case, you might ask yourself, is he stressed out because he is involved in causing harm to his child or his girlfriend and he is feeling guilt? Could he be feeling guilty because he feels he didn't do enough to protect them and make them safe? He might be feeling stress because of an overwhelming feeling of fear for the safety of his loved ones. Many people are terribly stressed when they are called on to speak in public. Mr. Carey was answering questions from a group of reporters armed with cameras and microphones that were broadcasting across the entire planet. Maybe a little stress there....

Our point is, when you are trying to diagnose human behavior, you can't always take any *one single thing* and draw a conclusion about what a person's behavior may mean. You must consider everything you know about the situation and the person.

Correctly understanding what a person's *current behavior* says about their *past behavior* is much more an art than a science.

"READING THE SCENE!"

Most of us have the ability to "read" a crime scene to some extent. You know, take the information your senses give you and combine that data with your education, experience, and perceptions to reach conclusions as to what happened. Things such as, is it a murder or a robbery, did the assailant break in the home, or were they allowed to enter as a trusted friend? Simple stuff like that. That was usually about all I could figure out!

At the other end of the spectrum were the magicians. Those gifted investigators who could soak it all up, digest it, analyze the information and come up with assumptions that were nothing short of amazing in their accuracy. They could consistently provide suggestions as to how a crime was committed and what type of person committed that crime. Information like this not only led to the discovery of prime suspects but helped interviewers decide how to approach the suspect during questioning.

TBI Special Agent William Warren Jones - we called him W.W. - was one of the gifted ones. Warren was born and raised in southern McNairy County, Tennessee. Buford Pusser country. A soon as he was old enough W.W. left the cotton patches, cornfields, and whiskey stills and went to work for the FBI in Washington D.C. He became an accomplished fingerprint expert before returning to Tennessee and becoming a member of the Tennessee Bureau of Criminal Identification, an agency that later became the Tennessee Bureau of Investigation.

Warren's hard work and dedication to duty were legendary. His thoroughness was unbelievable. He left no stone unturned. At the height of his career, Warren was involved in a terrible car crash. A McNairy deputy was killed and W.W. was seriously injured. Physically he was never quite the same, but mentally he was as sharp as ever.

Mr.Paul was a successful farmer in northern Gibson county. He was a nice fellow and was glad to help folks out when they were running a little short on money. Pay a small service charge and add a little "pinch", or "juice" (that's what they called the interest), and the money was yours! For a short amount of time. Usually about a week.

One sunny afternoon a neighbor went by to check on his friend Mr. Paul. The garage door had been broken into and when he peered inside, the neighbor saw Mr. Paul lying on the floor. He was dead.

The general appearance of the scene indicated a burglary that turned into a robbery, then a fight, and resulted in a murder. The house was ransacked and we assumed the killer was looking for the farmer's stash of cash. We proceeded to work the crime scene, taking photos and looking for whatever evidence or clues that might be present.

Jones was sitting at the kitchen table making notes and I walked over to talk to check in with him. 'What do you think W.W.?", I said, making conversation. "We're looking for a left-handed woman Jimmie Van" he calmly replied. I'm pretty sure my mouth almost dropped open. A left-handed woman? I thought. This is a frontal assault, full force violent robbery and murder. It is obviously a man-on-man crime. On top of that, I figured I was probably the one left-handed person within a five mile radius of that farm!

Well, I thought, everybody misses one every now and then. Even Babe Ruth struck out. I told W.W. I was going to go check on Joe Shepard and I would see him later. Even though I was sure Warren had missed the call, I knew him well enough to know better than to totally disregard what he had to say. I kept the thought in the back of my mind. A left-handed woman...

After about 3 weeks of long days and endless nights of hard work we got a break in the case and made an arrest. The killer confessed.

The murderer was a bald-headed, epileptic, left-handed lesbian. You can bet I was at the office first thing the next morning to buy Warren a cup of coffee and get a little training from the expert!

"OK W.W., lay it on me. How did you figure out that was a left-handed woman?"

Warren said, "First thing, you looked at the scene and said to yourself this was a violent crime and most violent crimes are committed by men. Most men are right-handed. Both these things were probably good assumptions if you are strictly depending on statistics. You can't necessarily do that when dealing with these situations. When you first look at a scene, you got to be totally open-minded and take whatever information that scene is giving you. You can plug in stats and probabilities later on."

He continued. "You remember the door the killer broke though, the one that went from the garage into the kitchen? The top half of that door was glass and was separated into small rectangular panels. The intruder broke out the panel that was level with and directly to the left of the doorknob/lock. That made it easy to reach in with the *left hand* and unlock the door. It would have been much easier for a *right-handed* person to go about two panels higher up on the door, break out the panel, reach in with the *right hand* and reach straight down to the lock. Simple."

"OK", I said sheepishly replied. "I get that. Makes perfect sense now that you explain it. But what indicated it was a female?"

Warren patiently explained. "When the killer searched the house looking for money, it was too nice. A man would have been in a hurry to find the cash and get away from that house. Stuff would have been slung all over the place, drawers thrown in the floor, furniture turned over. That's not what we saw. Think back to what the master bedroom looked like. There was a dresser against the wall. If you faced the dresser, the bed was directly behind you. When the searcher removed the clothing from the dresser, the stuff was piled in neat stacks on the bed. A man would not have done that. He would have just dumped it all on the floor and looked for the money!"

It was so simple but so smart. I was too involved with trying to gather information too quickly and maybe come up with some incredible clue! I should have simply, slowed down and tried to actually "read" what I was seeing!

Key Issues

- Always view the crime scene. Even if it's a cold case that is years old. Do your best to get a "feel" for the scene. What did it look like to victims, witnesses, and suspects? At some point, turn your back to the scene and look around. What is the view from that perspective?
- Just look and then stop!! Don't touch anything until everything has been photographed and properly collected. Once a crime scene or piece of evidence is disturbed - we referred to it as being contaminated - it can't be fixed. It may be ruined so far being used in court. It drives me nuts when I see these TV detectives run in and start grabbing guns and shell casings and such. If that was one of MY scenes, there might have been a second murder to work after I shot that nut that botched the evidence.

My great friend Warren Jones went on to a better place many years ago but the wonderful memories, great stories,

love, respect, and friendship will last forever.
   Rest in Peace, W.W.

   Jim Leach
   November 2020

"A DIFFERENT LIMB"

Western Mental Health Institution in Bolivar Tennessee was the largest employer in Hardeman County. The good paying state jobs were considered the best employment opportunity in the area. The Institution maintained a large footprint in the small town and the administrators were well respected community leaders.

When someone mentioned the town of Bolivar, one of two things came to mind. Sports fans immediately thought of outstanding athletes. Others thought about "Western". The comment that "They had to carry Aunt Linda to Bolivar", meant Aunt Linda was suffering from a little more than normal confusion and perhaps having an occasional conversation with someone the rest of couldn't quite see or hear.

There was minimal security at the hospital, and that appeared to be all that was needed. Patients didn't escape, they simply walked off. Local police would find them shuffling down the side of the road and gently pick them up and carry them back to their temporary home. Softball was popular and the City's softball fields bordered the hospital property. A few patients were regular visitors to the games. The fans knew them by name and enjoyed visiting with the friendly hospital residents.

In one terrible afternoon, everything changed.

Don Clifton was the Chief of Police in Bolivar. He left the Memphis Police Department to take the position. Having worked in Memphis in the 1960s and 70's Don knew how to investigate crime. That afternoon he found me at the courthouse. "Leach, I need you to go out to Western with me". "OK", I said, "What's going on?" "I'm not sure", he replied, "but it doesn't sound good. Come on."

Luzon was waiting on us when we got to the hospital. He was head of security and a good solid man, who knew his business well. On this afternoon, he was noticeably different. His normally calm demeanor was gone. He was visibly upset. "I'm sure glad you fellows got here". I got to show you something."

Looking at the front of the property from Highway 64, you viewed many large medieval looking buildings that housed hospital staff and patients. We were about to discover there was an area behind the structures that included many acres of woods and pasture. Apparently, this area was used by some of the patients as kind of a party area. We found whiskey bottles, beer cans, candy wrappers and there was even a pair of underwear hanging from a tree limb!

At the back of the recreation yard, Luzon showed us a group of human footprints leading toward the backside property. We followed the tracks, at one point traveling about a hundred yards down a sand ditch.

Eventually, the tracks stopped. There, partially hidden underneath some tree limbs, we found Barney's lifeless body.

Doctors described Barney as being catatonic. He simply stood in the yard and stared, apparently oblivious to his surroundings. He showed no response to any type of stimulus. Poor Barney was just *there*. He existed.

Our investigation revealed a very simple and straightforward case. Five patients began to visit with Barney in the afternoons every so often. What started out as playful conduct, probably designed just to "have something to do", soon escalated into acts of sexual aggression.

After a while, the group got tired of playing like this and decided it would be fun to beat Barney while they sodomized him. Then somebody decided to choke him. According to their statements, they all participated in all the acts. Of course, the excited choking resulted in the death of Barney.

The American justice system is set up to see that things are done legally. Sometimes it seems our preoccupation with making sure what we do is *legal*, conflicts with making sure what we do is *right*. In this case, we felt it was imperative to not only run a legal investigation but also see that the *right* thing was done in the end.

It is very doubtful these guys really understood the concept of *murder*. They knew something wrong had been done that could get them in trouble. This truth is evidenced by the fact they went to great lengths to try and hide Barney's body.

Normal investigative technique was utilized. Each witness was questioned independently so that whatever his buddy said would not influence what *he* said when we asked questions. The patients gave surprisingly clear and accurate statements. Something very exciting had happened in their life and they were anxious to tell us about it!

Hospital staff had not seen any abusive behavior, but some could testify the small group had regularly been seen "hanging around" Barney.

After taking statements from each suspect, we asked each one of them, separately, to show us where they left Barney. They walked us straight to the spot.

At the end of every interview, the last question was, "Is there anything else you would like to tell us?" When we asked the first suspect we talked to, David, this last question, he said, "Yeah. One limb was different." Chief Clifton and I froze in our seats and looked at each other. This was huge in building statement credibility. We had never mentioned the limb, which came from a cherry tree. Reviewing the tape of the statement, you could easily hear how shocked we were. When David mentioned the limb, the silence was deafening.

Later on, some people would try to say we "led" these guys and told them what to say in their statements. We couldn't have told David to say this, even if we had wanted. Frankly, with all that was going on, I didn't even notice the "different" limb.

Three of the five patients involved told us about the limb. When we visited the scene, four of them actually picked up the branch and handed it to us. It gave immediate credibility to our investigation.

There was an ominous cloud hanging over our community. People were waiting for us to finish and tell them what happened. Some would ask us how it was going. Most seemed to avoid us. Perhaps they feared what we might tell them. Had Bolivar been misled all these years into believing the residents were harmless? Had Western been harboring potential killers all this time? Should they keep the children inside? Were new door locks needed?

Nothing is quite so frightening as the unknown.

The District Attorney was a guy named Mike Whitaker and he would eventually decide as to how we would proceed once our investigation was complete. He was a fine prosecutor and an even finer person.

Basically, the case could be handled in two ways. General Whitaker could convene a special session of the grand jury, and in a secret hearing, have investigators explain to the grand jurors what happened. The Grand Jury would then decide as to whether to dismiss the accusations or indict the suspect and send the case to Circuit Court for trial. Once again, Grand Jury proceedings are secret, so the public would not hear the evidence.

The other option was for me to go to the courthouse, sign warrants on the suspects, and give them a preliminary hearing in open General Sessions court.

That's what we did. The courtroom was packed. All the defendants were present in the courtroom. It was plain to see these folks were not monsters.

They were not as fortunate as the rest of us. All they knew was their life had been shattered and they were terrified by what was happening.

Eventually, the court decided the defendants were not competent to stand trial.

This case brought unusual challenges and at times we had to "think outside the box".

Key Issues

- In any investigation, it is critical that certain aspects remain confidential. These facts must be known only to the criminal(s) who perpetrated the crime and investigators assigned to the case. When a witness or suspect talks about those facts, it can be assumed they are a *genuine* source of information. Utilizing this tactic can also guard against an investigator being duped by a fabricated statement or a false confession.

- From the time a case is initiated, investigators must begin preparing to go to trial, if necessary. All evidence must be collected legally so it can be submitted in court. This includes statements and confessions. Memory and comprehension may come into question when testimony is offered from the witness stand. Understanding this, investigators may ask questions showing the witness's ability. A good interviewer should speak to a prosecutor to get an idea of questions to ask that might demonstrate a clear thinking process.
- Never, ever, neglect to ask the final question. There are many different ways to phrase the request, but basically what you are trying to do is to get the person to tell you *anything* they may be thinking about the case. A short explanation will help the person to feel comfortable opening up to you.

"I know I have asked you a lot of questions and you are probably tired of answering them! Please stay with me for just another minute. Even though I've asked you a lot, I can't think of everything and I feel sure I may have forgotten some things. I want you to take a minute and think back. Is there anything you can think of that you can tell me that we haven't already talked about? Do me a favor and don't try and decide whether or not what you have to say is important. Let me make that decision. There may be things about the case that I know and you don't! A small bit of information that you think doesn't   matter, could be incredibly important to me."

You may be amazed at what you may hear. Remember, if that question had not been asked in the Western Mental Health Institute murder case, the "different limb" might not have been mentioned and the suspect's credibility would have forever been in question.

IS THE HOLLY BOBO INVESTIGATION A "COLD CASE"?

Yes. It is.

Most of the time when an investigation is referred to as a "cold case" it refers to a homicide. When I have been hired by departments to work on these cases, we only looked at those that were one year old or older. In the practical world of working murder cases, we considered the case to be getting old if we didn't have someone in custody, or at least, a good suspect within 72 hours of the discovery of the crime.

There is one primary reason why cold cases become cold cases. They are HARD TO SOLVE. Witnesses forget - or at least claim they forgot. Many times they may suffer from substance abuse or mental illness and trying to get an accurate description of events becomes more difficult over a longer period of time. Important witnesses may have died or moved and can be very hard to locate. The chain of evidence may be poor for a variety of reasons. These are just a few of the issues that make cold cases difficult to solve and we will look at some of them in more depth in later articles.

Basically, there are a few ways for an investigator to get involved in a cold case investigation. They could have been the investigator in the initial investigation and new evidence has been developed or a case review or department policy demands that the investigation be revived. Other ways an investigator may get involved is because the agency wants a "fresh set of eyes" to look at the case, or you are hired to specifically investigate this case or several cold cases. Sometimes police departments or sheriff's departments ask a state or federal agency to look at a cold case. Investigators with local departments are covered up with incidents that occur every day and just can't devote the time they would like investigating a cold case.

The first thing you need to try and do is understand the case. Of course, you want to read and organize everything in the file. This can be pretty frustrating, especially if the case is several years old. For example, there may be notes written on restaurant napkins that really look interesting. The problem is, you have no idea who wrote the note! You have to take the note around to officers who may have worked "back then" and see if they have ever heard this information, or, maybe they can recognize the handwriting. Believe it or not, laptops did not always exist and reports weren't quite as good 30 years ago as they are today.

In reviewing the file, you may find prime suspects. People who had means, motive, and opportunity to commit the murder. You must DO YOUR BEST to either clear a prime suspect or else, prosecute them. Too often you cannot do either one and years later you still wonder if the person who appeared to be a prime suspect might have actually been the killer. That is a very troubling thought for the victim's survivors as well as the investigators. The most high-profile case that comes to mind is the investigation into the death of Jon Benet Ramsey. There has been speculation for many years that the little girl's parents may have been responsible for her death.

When someone is murdered, especially if it is a high-profile case or it involves more than one jurisdiction, there may be too many police involved. That may sound strange, but it is very true. One group of investigators may not know what another group of investigators is doing. This situation can cause multiple problems. The same witness may be interviewed about the same information 2-3 times. A witness can quickly grow tired of this and become uncooperative. If there are different agencies involved, there may be several representatives speaking to the media and this can make it appear there are differing opinions as to the progress of the investigation. Problems of this nature may erode public confidence in law enforcement and that is terribly damaging to the case.

In the beginning, when the case is hot, everybody is talking to one another every day. A month after the killing, investigators from other departments are forced to take care of cases in their own jurisdiction. Information developed by another agency may not always get passed along to investigators responsible for working on the murder. There is no malice involved or no intent to impede the investigation, it is just human nature. The information is developed and the investigator who obtained the new evidence thinks, "I need to call Jim (the homicide case investigator) tomorrow and tell him about this." The problem is, that night, the investigator who developed the new lead catches a fresh homicide and must get busy on that case. Many times the information never gets passed along to Jim.

Connie Sue House's body was discovered in Madison County Tennessee. The investigation proved she was abducted from Milan, carried to Crockett County, and then she was found in Madison County. Tennessee Highway Patrol Investigator Paul Dunaway was assigned the case several years after the murder. A meeting was put together to review the investigation and everyone who had worked on the original investigation was asked to attend and bring copies of any paperwork they had on the case. Of course, once everyone got together and started talking, there was some information developed that was not in the case files. Thoughts, ideas, and opinions, even though they may not be admissible in court, can be tremendously valuable in an investigation but may not be put in the file because they are not facts.

Dunaway spent all weekend going over the information gathered in the meeting. When he put it all together, he had a case ready to go to the Grand Jury! Instead, he and another THP /CID investigator Frankie Floied traveled to California to interview one of the future defendants. After obtaining a statement from him, they returned to Tennessee, and eventually, two people were convicted for the murder of Ms. House.

Another situation occurs when a prime suspect is developed or maybe even be arrested. Many times this can stimulate further investigation since you now have a photograph of the suspect as well as fingerprints, DNA, and maybe a statement to analyze. When Kenneth O'Guinn was arrested for the murder of Sheila Cupples, his photograph was included in a photo line-up and showed to several witnesses. One of the witnesses identified O'Guinn as a person he saw escorting Sheila to a vehicle on the night of her disappearance. This testimony, along with O'Guinn's confession and some other evidence, resulted in his conviction for First Degree Murder and he later died on death row.

A big issue when investigating cold cases can be witness memory. Some of the things affecting memory include how well the brain receives the information and how effectively the brain retrieves the information. The length of time the brain retains the information may also greatly affect the accuracy of the recollection and obviously, this is a factor in a cold case.

There is a good chance some, or all of these issues will be present in the Holly Bobo murder trial. Reports indicate the prosecution may call as many as 200 witnesses.

In other developments regarding the Bobo case, the state says evidence will be produced showing Holly may have been killed by a firearm. A wound mark discovered on the victim's skull is said to be consistent with a bullet hole. Also, the defense claims there was a footprint found at the Bobo home, the site of Holly's abduction. Defense attorneys want to examine this possible evidence. Prosecutors say the footprint does not exist.

The trial is set to begin on September 11 and jury selection will commence on September 9. Zach Adams will be the first of 3 defendants to be tried.

THE DIFFERENT PHASES OF THE HOLLY BOBO TRIAL   9/10/17

Holly Bobo, a beautiful 20 year old nursing student, was abducted from her home in rural Decatur County Tennessee in April of 2011.   It was said a man dressed in camouflage clothing led her into the woods behind her home. A massive manhunt and investigation ensued. Volunteers from several states searched for Holly for many weeks with no success.

In September of 2014, her skeletal remains were discovered a few miles from where she was abducted. Three men were charged with her abduction and murder. Several people have been granted immunity and it is assumed they will provide testimony for the prosecution. On Memorial Day weekend of 2017, a gun was recovered and authorities indicate they will connect it to the crime.

The prosecution says they will introduce many items of evidence in the trial and they have requested 200 subpoenas for possible witnesses. The defense has said their case should take about a week to present. This is a death penalty case which means if the defendant is convicted, there will be a separate hearing to determine what the punishment will be. The jury will have to decide between a life sentence with the possibility of parole, a life sentence without the possibility of parole, or death by execution.

The defendant in this trial is Zach Adams.

Jury selection took place on Saturday, September 9th. During this phase, the judge and attorneys for both the prosecution and the defense had the opportunity to question potential jurors. They aimed to pick jurors who can be fair and impartial and will reach their decision based solely on the evidence presented in court. If close attention is paid to the questions the lawyers asked, we may begin to get an idea of the theory each side will try and prove during the trial. 15 jurors were picked to hear the case, including 12 primary jurors and 3 alternates. An alternate listens to the case, just like those who are sitting on the jury and an alternate may be placed on the jury should one of the jurors be excused for some reason.

Opening arguments from each side are scheduled to be made to the jury on Monday the 11th. At this time the attorneys will describe what evidence they plan to introduce during the trial. The prosecution will explain their theory of how Holly was abducted, assaulted, and eventually murdered and how they know the defendant committed these crimes... The defense attorneys will try and convince the jurors their client did not commit the crimes and may even introduce their theory of what happened and direct the jury's attention toward another suspect or some unknown other suspect.

The prosecution will be allowed to present their case first and will introduce whatever physical evidence they may have as well as witness testimony. The defense has the opportunity to challenge the evidence the prosecution introduced. The defense may question such things as the relevance the evidence has to the crime, the chain of custody of the evidence, and any expert testimony concerning tests that were performed on the evidence. The defense also can cross-examine all prosecution witnesses and challenge their truthfulness and the integrity of their testimony. Expect the defense to vigorously question the honesty of testimony from accomplices or people who may have been "accessories" (these can be people who aided in the perpetration of the crime but did not directly participate). Testimony from jail inmates and close friends or family members may also come under close scrutiny. We can expect the defense to ask investigators about any other people who were developed as suspects or may have been arrested and released. The defense will want to know what evidence existed to make these people become a suspect and what happened in the investigation that "cleared" them.

   The defense will present their case once the prosecution finishes presenting theirs and will go through basically the same process the state (prosecution) went through in the trial's beginning. The defense can present any evidence they may have as well as witness testimony. The prosecution can challenge anything the defense brings up, just like the defense questioned the state's case.

Closing arguments are the last phase of the presentment of both side's cases. Remember, in their opening arguments the prosecution and the defense told the jury what they intended to prove. In the closing arguments, they sort of say, "See, I told you I was going to prove my case, and I did it!" They will then proceed to remind the jurors of evidence and witness testimony that was favorable to their case. The prosecution tells their side first, then the defense presents their version, and then finally, the prosecution is allowed to argue their side one last time to the jury.   The prosecution has an opportunity to present a summary and address the jury for the last time before they go into deliberations.

Sometimes there is a little leeway in these arguments. I was testifying as a TBI Agent in a large theft of property case and the defense attorney began describing my testimony to the jury in his closing arguments. After a few minutes, I leaned over and asked another Agent, who was in the courtroom when I testified if I had said the things the defense attorney said that I had said. My partner said I had not testified to those things (I was pretty sure I hadn't!). The prosecution lawyers did not object, so the defense attorney got away with lying to the jury about what I said in my testimony! I guess the jury "caught it" because they convicted the guy.

The judge's charge is the last thing the jury will hear before going into deliberations. The judge will make sure they understand what criminal offenses the defendant is charged with and exactly what it takes to convict the defendant of those particular crimes. In other words, the judge defines the "elements" of the crime or crimes. The judge will also admonish the jurors to base their decision on the evidence they have heard in the trial and nothing else. If any evidence or testimony was not admitted in the trial presentation, it cannot legally be considered by the jurors in their decision.

Jury deliberation is the final phase in deciding the guilt or innocence of the accused person. The men and women of the jury consider all the evidence they have heard that was legally entered into the trial. The judge will have instructed them to disregard anything that they heard or saw that was later ruled inadmissible.

Of course, it is questionable how well the jurors can rule out things they heard from witnesses that were later ruled by the judge to be inadmissible. In one trial I was involved in, the defense called in a person as a character witness for the defendant. Upon cross-examination, the prosecution asked the witness if he had ever seen the defendant do anything "strange". The witness, trying to be honest, said, "One time I saw him when he ate a cat". The judge immediately excused the jury and asked them to step out of the courtroom while everyone regained their composure. Even though the judge did all he could to keep this unexpected testimony from contaminating the jury, it may have stayed in their minds when they were deliberating the case.

Experts often disagree about what can be interpreted by the length of time the jury deliberates or "stays out". Many different factors may influence the time factor and that makes it difficult to make a good interpretation. Some say a short jury deliberation is an indication they believed the prosecution's case and reached a quick guilty verdict. Other experts say exactly the opposite. Years ago we tried a law enforcement official and several of his accomplices in federal court. The case was given to the jury at lunchtime. An FBI Agent, and a DEA Agent, and I went to lunch together. As we were returning to the courthouse, we could see the windows on the outside of the jury deliberation room, and jurors were looking out the windows and standing up talking to one another. It appeared obvious they were through discussing the case. We felt this was a sign they had reached a not guilty verdict because they had finished so quickly. We were wrong. The jury convicted all 16 defendants on a total of 172 counts.

The sentencing phase takes place if the defendant is convicted of a First Degree Murder charge that carries the death penalty. Simply put, the prosecution will try and convince the jury the convicted killer deserves to be executed by the state and the defense will try and convince the jury that the killer should not be executed. Guilt has already been decided. Both sides can introduce evidence such as prior criminal acts, family history, and religious beliefs. These types of evidence would probably not have been brought out in the initial trial phase. Emotion may play a large part in hearings of this nature.

If the defendant is sentenced to death, there will automatically be an appeals process that will take years to complete. I gave a deposition in 1995 in the case against Robert Glen Coe and he had been convicted in the early 1980s. In another death penalty case, I testified in a deposition in federal court in 1993 against Kenneth O'Guinn and he was convicted in the mid-1980s. Coe was eventually executed and O'Guinn died on death row.

We will be following the Holly Bobo case closely.

Let's hope that justice is served and our system works as it should.

As the slogan in front of the TBI headquarters in Nashville says, "That Innocence Not Suffer. Nor Guilt Escape". That sums it up better than anything else I can say

BOBO TRIAL - DAY 1   9/12/17

In opening arguments yesterday the prosecution alleged that Zach Adams, the defendant currently on trial, told his friend Jason Autry about kidnapping and raping Holly Bobo. Prosecutors say

Adams also told Autry that Shayne Austin and Dylan Adams were accomplices in these crimes. Dylan Adams is Zach Adams' brother and Austin committed suicide. Jason Autry has been given immunity in exchange for his truthful testimony. Dylan Adams also cooperated with authorities.

Autry told prosecutors Holly was covered up with a blanket in Zach Adams' truck and the killers, thinking she was already dead, were headed to throw her body into the Tennessee River near Birdsong. Autry says Adams talked about "gutting" the victim. That is known as a way to release the gasses that collect in a body from accumulating and causing the body to float to the surface. Anyone who watches all the "crime shows" on television has been educated in this method of disposing of a body. Evidently, for some reason, it was decided to dispose of the body in another fashion other than throwing the victim in the river. When it was discovered Holly was still alive, Zach got a gun and shot her in the head. Austin says Adams bragged about how pretty his victim was and how much fun it had been to assault and murder her.

Defense attorneys say Zach Adams is not the killer and cite the fact that investigators had picked other suspects before deciding Adams was guilty. The defense alleges that even Holly's brother was a suspect at one time. They say Dylan Adams has limited mental capability and cooperated after being manipulated by the police.

An unusual twist occurred when Karen Bobo, Holly's mother, testified she knew all three men who were arrested for her daughter's murder and was Adam's fourth-grade teacher. Ms. Bobo collapsed on the witness stand after she identified her daughter's purse, wallet, and a sandwich she made for Holly the day she disappeared. Police recovered these items during the investigation. After her collapse, Karen was able to regain her composure and

return to the witness stand. Defense
attorneys asked for a mistrial due to her
collapse on the witness stand in front of
the jury but their motion was denied.

Holly's brother, Clint Bobo, testified
he saw his sister walking into the woods
with a man dressed in camouflage
clothing who he thought was her
boyfriend at about 7:30 am on the day
she disappeared. A neighbor also heard
sounds that could have been described
as a woman screaming around the same
time.

Several things could be significant
depending on what future testimony
reveals.

The locations where Holly's personal
items were recovered could be
important if these items were found
near the defendant's home or they
were found in a fairly direct route
between the area of her abduction and
the defendant's home or another
location the prosecution can prove she
was held by her abductors.

The blanket Austin says Holly was hidden underneath in Adam's truck has the potential to be relevant. If the blanket was recovered, it might produce hair and fiber evidence from the victim. Also, if the blanket is unique enough, and Austin's description of it was detailed enough, the defendants' mere possession of the blanket could be incriminating. Of course, Austin and Adams were friends so it could be argued that Austin could have seen the blanket at Adams's house any time.   In a case I worked on years ago, two girls from Corinth Mississippi were abducted, sexually assaulted, tied up, and left to die in the woods in Hardeman County Tennessee. They described a very unique seat cover in the truck the kidnapper was traveling in when he abducted them. We were able to recover the seat cover and the girls identified it in court. The identification was instrumental in convicting their attacker. Of course in the Bobo case, several years passed from the time of the murder until the time that police knew anything about the blanket or knew where to look for it. This time lapse gave the killers ample time to destroy the evidence.

Autry tells about a gunshot to Holly's head. We know from earlier testimony that experts will testify her skull had suffered an injury that was similar to a gunshot wound and we know a gun that may have been involved in the crime was recovered. It remains to be seen if the gun can be tied to the gunshot wound to the skull or if the gun can be linked to the defendant.

The one definite "time" that has been determined in the case is when Holly was abducted. If the defense could convince the jury that Adams was somewhere else at that particular time, it would indicate his innocence. I think it would be a good assumption that investigators checked all pertinent databases such as criminal histories and driver license histories to make sure he wasn't locked up, at work, or got a speeding ticket in another state on the same morning she disappeared. Defense attorneys are supposed to let the prosecution know if they intend to enter evidence concerning any "alibi" they may try to use as a defense.

As we discussed in an earlier article, the defense is going to ask the prosecution what happened with other people who were developed as suspects and later cleared of any involvement. The defense will try and convince the jury that one of these suspects actually committed the murder and not their client.

It appears, at this point, the biggest question will be how well Autry does when he testifies. If you look at earlier articles in "The Leach Report" you will see discussions of ways to form an opinion as to whether witnesses are being truthful. The attorneys will utilize these techniques – and more – to try and convince the jury that Autry is lying or telling the truth, depending on which side of the issue they represent. If Autry is very convincing, it may force Adams to take the witness and testify to rebut Autry's testimony. Defense attorneys probably don't want to put their client on the witness stand.

BOBO TRIAL - THE PROSECUTION 9/17/17

Tennessee Highway Patrol Lieutenant Warren Rainey spoke of interviewing Zach Adams. Lt. Rainey describes Adams as being nervous and running back to the house when the interview ended. Rainey also tells of a mattress leaning up against the house and Rainey says this looked so unusual to him that he had a "gut instinct" that something was wrong.

Two other witnesses describe Adams washing, vacuuming, and blowing off the mattresses. One of these witnesses says he saw 2 mattresses and this witness also describes Adams spending over an hour vacuuming his truck. This activity occurred immediately after Lt. Rainey left the Adams home.

FBI Special Agent Matt Ross testified to an interview he conducted on April 23, 2011, with Adams at Adam's residence. This was 10 days after Holly's disappearance. During the interview, SA Ross noticed scratches on Adams' arm. With Adams' permission, Ross took photographs of these scratches. Adams also let SA Ross look around his home. Ross said he had received a tip that Adams might be a person of interest. In this initial interview, Adams said he got up that day about 10-10:30 and went to a gas station with his brother, Dylan, (also charged in the murder) and a friend.

Zach Adams' former girlfriend, Rebecca Earp, says she stayed with Adams the night before Holly's disappearance. She says Adams left the house between 6 - 7:30 am saying he had to haul away some scrap metal. She became concerned later that morning when Adams called her using his brother's phone, not his own (if true, this would indicate the two brothers were together). When Adams returned home later that morning, she noticed scratches on his arm and neck. Earp confronted Adams and told him she did not believe he had hauled away scrap that morning. Earp testified, "He said he would tie me up just like he did Holly Bobo and nobody would ever see me again." Earp told defense attorneys she did not report this information to the police because she was scared.

Witnesses testified to discovering several personal items belonging to Holley including her purse and lunch box, the SIM card belonging to her cell phone, a cell phone believed to be hers, a pair of pink panties, and a balled-up piece of paper with her name and address written on it. All of these items were found in different places, but, they were all near the property of Shayne Austin. Shayne Austin was arrested for the murder and later committed suicide.

TBI forensic scientist Laura Hodge described the crime scene search. An inhaler, 2 purses, keys with the letter "H", and cosmetic items as well as a wallet with Holly's driver's license were found near the skeletal remains. She testified to recovering a .410 gauge shotgun shell and a .32 caliber pistol shell casing. Dr. Marco Ross conducted the autopsy and testified that the cause of death was definitely a gunshot wound and probably a .32 caliber weapon. He said it could have been a smaller caliber, but definitely was not a larger caliber. The weapon recovered is a revolver and if the shell casing is the one involved in Holley's murder, that is confusing. The killer would have had to remove the one shell casing from the gun and drop it out with the body. It doesn't make much sense, but sometimes these things don't make much sense.

Jason Autry testified on day 4 of the trial. At the beginning of his testimony, prosecutors made sure the jury was aware this witness had flaws. He told the jury he was a former drug addict and had been in jail on drug and theft charges several times. To summarize his story, he says he contacted Zach Adams by phone a little before 9 am on the morning of Holly's disappearance. He was calling Adams to buy dope. Adams said he was busy, but later called Autry back and said he (Adams) needed help. Autry thought he needed help cooking a batch of methamphetamine. Upon his arrival at Shayne Autry's house (where he met Adams), Adams said he needed help in disposing of the dead body of Holly Bobo. Shayne Austin and Dylan Adams were both present. Holly was wrapped in a blanket in the back of Zach's truck and Zach and Jason headed to dispose of the body. It was Jason's idea to disembowel her and throw her in the Tennessee River so the turtles would eat her body. Autry said he knew of this method of body disposal being used 11 years before. Once they arrived at the river, they discovered she was still alive. There was a small amount of blood on the blanket and the truck. Autry never looked inside the blanket. Autry made sure there was no one around. He let Adams know there were no witnesses and then Autry heard one shot fired and that's when Zach Adams killed Holly Bobo. The pair feared some people boating on the river had heard the shot and seen them, so they fled the area. Autry told Adams he had to leave to meet his girlfriend for lunch.

He met with the Adams brothers and Austin about 2 pm. There were problems between the killers and finally there was a fight between Shayne and Zach. Victor Dinsmore broke up the fight and Zach later said he had hidden his truck at Dinsmore's garage. Autry says he and Austin traded the murder weapon to Dinsmore for some pills. Dinsmore later showed where the pistol had been thrown away. Autry was shown the pistol police recovered and he said it looked like the gun Adams used to kill Holly. Austin was wearing the pistol on his side when Autry showed up at the house. Autry mentioned someone was mowing the grass when he met up with the three defendants and one of the killers said a satellite system installer was supposed to come by that morning. Autry testified Adams was wearing camouflage clothing that day. Autry also told a story about going to the place where Adams said the body was dumped. The area was located on someone's property, not the refuge. To go on the property without raising suspicion he pretended to be going fishing. When he asked a lady's permission to go fishing on their property, she told Autry he would have to get permission from her father, and her father was gone to search for Holly Bobo. Autry became so distraught at the mention of Holly's name the lady reported the incident to police.

Adams gave Autry two stories about how he targeted Holly. On the day of the murder, Adams told Autry he knew

Natalie Bobo, a cousin of Holly's who worked in a strip club. Rebecca Earp testified she introduced the two to one another. Natalie told Adams that Holly might be interested in having sex with them. In August of 2012, Adams told a different story. He said, "they" (Zach, Dylan, and Shayne) went to the Bobo home to teach Holly's brother how to make meth. Adams said Holly came out screaming at them and so they took her. Holly's brother Clint testified to seeing one person.

Adams's conversation with Autry also confirmed Zach Adams, Shayne Autry, and Dylan Adams raped Holly. Adams told Autry that Dylan performed sex on Zach and Shayne before raping Holly. Allegedly the rape took place in a barn belonging to Shayne Austin's grandfather. It is possible there could have other rapes since mattresses were seen being cleaned up outside the house. Some of Holly's personal effects were found near this barn.

A few days after the murder Zach made a deal for Autry to kill his brother, Dylan. Zach said Dylan had not slept since the crime and Zach was probably afraid Dylan might start running his mouth. Autry carried Dylan out on the river and was going to kill him and dump the body in the river. The plan fell apart when a man who knew Dylan encountered them and Autry knew he could be identified. That ended the murder plot.

Autry told defense attorneys he didn't tell police the truth initially because he feared for his safety and the safety of his family and he feared it would hurt his relationship with his girlfriend.

In talking to journalists and law enforcement officers who watched Autry testify, I hear differing opinions about how well he did on the stand. Some said he did a great job and was very believable. Others said he appeared arrogant or tried to be "cute". Two people told me he used words that did not seem to be his own which lead them to believe he may have been "coached" in his testimony.   I bring this up to point out that different people watching the same testimony had differing opinions. Autry's testimony is obviously the backbone of the prosecution's case. The point I am trying to make is, the twelve people on the jury may have differing opinions as to Autry's credibility as well, and their perception is the only one that matters.

The prosecution would like to be able to confirm *anything* Jason Autry says as being the truth since that would make his whole testimony more believable. The single gunshot is consistent with the forensic scientist's testimony. According to Austin, Adams said all three of the men raped Holly. The testimony concerning the mattresses being cleaned provides some corroboration for the allegation of sexual assault. On day five of the trial, Dinsmore confirmed he broke up the fight between Shayne and Zach and that he hid Zach Adams's truck. A lady working in the area testified she saw Dinsmore talking to 3 men between 2:30 pm- 3:30 pm. She identified Jason Autry as being one of the three men. Dinsmore also testified he traded drugs for the gun he later suspected was used to kill Holly. Dinsmore was given immunity to testify because he is a convicted felon and it would be illegal for him to be in possession of a firearm. So far, there has been no implication that he was involved in the murder. The parts of Autry's testimony concerning someone mowing the grass and installing satellite service were confirmed by investigators.

On day 6 of the trial TBI Agent Mike Frizzell said cell phone records showed at 7:42 am Holly made her last call on her cell phone and she was near her home when she made the call. After that, there were many incoming calls and text messages that went unanswered. The final ping from her phone came at 9:25 am from the same area where the phone and SIM card were recovered. This is near Shayne Austin's home where Autry met Zach, Dylan, and Shayne. Zach Adams's phone pinged in the same area at 8:19 am. Both Zach and Holly's phones were in that area until 9:42 am. The cell phones of both Zach Adams and Jason Autry pinged the cell tower in the Birdsong area between 9:42 am and 10:30 am. This is the area where Autry testified Holly was murdered. These times are consistent with Autry's testimony.

Also, on day 6, a friend of Holly's, Candace Wood, told of a double date she and Holly and their boyfriends took together. They went to the World's Largest Coon Hunt at the Decatur County Fairgrounds. She noticed a man who was paying very close attention to them. She caught him staring many times and he would look away when she looked at him. It bothered her enough she suggested they leave. A few days after Holly disappeared she went to the police. A sketch artist was brought in and she provided the artist details to draw a picture of the man who had been staring at Holly. The picture the artist drew was Shayne Austin. She could not have seen a picture of Austin in the media since he wasn't even developed as a suspect until years later.

TBI Agent Brent Booth testified that Zach Adams, Jason Autry, Shayne Autry, and Dylan Adams were developed as possible suspects early in the investigation but the leads were not followed up as well as they could have been.

The prosecution is expected to finish its case on Monday, the seventh day of the trial. The prosecution says they plan to introduce 2 more witnesses and it is a safe assumption these witnesses will back-up the testimony of Autry and/ or other prosecution witnesses.

The defense will begin that afternoon or Tuesday morning, depending on when the prosecution rests and what the judge decides to do.

In a case of this nature, common defense tactics may include; attacking the investigators, attacking prosecution witnesses, and even attacking the victim. A more detailed description of what the defense's attack plan could be will be posted Monday morning.

The prosecution did a very good job. Now it's the defense's turn.

BOBO TRIAL - DEFENSE TACTICS - 9/18/17

There are some issues that have been entered into evidence the defense can bring up questions about because they are not criminal acts in and of themselves but merely circumstantial evidence. In other words, the prosecution has to explain why they are important and relevant. The state's lawyers must fit the act into their theory of what happened and so far they have done a good job of doing this. Now the defense is going to provide an alternative theory about this evidence and try and convince the jury the acts or testimony are just fine to talk about, but they have nothing whatsoever to do with the case! I refer to this as the "*So What?* "defense tactic. I will give you some examples of what I am talking about that we may hear in the Bobo case.

Adams had mattresses leaned up against the house and he was seen cleaning them. *So What?* The defense may produce evidence saying this is a common practice in rural west Tennessee. I can just hear somebody testifying and saying, "Doesn't everybody air out their mattresses in the spring and clean them? My grandmother said it makes the mattresses last longer."

They say he had scratches on his arm and maybe his neck. *So What?* He mentioned hauling scrap and that kind of work could easily get a man scratched up!

Adams is a drug dealer and probably a drug addict. *So What?* Does that make him a kidnapper, rapist, and murderer?

Somebody saw him vacuuming out his truck. *So What?* He may have been hunting or met somebody in the middle of nowhere to do a dope deal and got stuck. You know a man's got to keep his truck clean!

Adams hid his truck out at Victor Dinsmore's place. *So What?* Everybody knows he owed Bobby money on a dope deal and Bobby told Betty he was going to take Adam's truck if Adam didn't pay up. Oh yeah, there was that deal with the title pawn place, too. They were also looking for Adams' truck because of what he owed them.

During an argument, he told his former girlfriend he would do her like he did Holly Bobo if she didn't shut up. *So What?* Don't most men (and women!) sometimes get mad and say crazy things they don't mean? Especially if they are strung out on drugs.

OK, you get the idea. Get ready to hear these types of things from the witness stand. This is totally legitimate and it may be the real answer. These attorneys are not going to introduce testimony they know is false. They are too professional for that. It is their job to present their client's case and then the jury must put together everything they have heard and seen and decide what the truth is.

As long as it is kept within reason and doesn't get too hateful, defense attorneys are pretty safe to try and discredit prosecution witnesses without alienating the jury.

Rebecca Earp gave some testimony that could be significant concerning the scratches on Zach Adams's arm and neck. Of course, the defense will bring it back to the jury's attention that she is a former girlfriend and may harbor ill will toward Adams. Also, all she can say is she saw some scratches, she doesn't really know how he got them. There might be a witness who will come forward to testify that Zach Adams had those scratches several days before Holly's disappearance. It would not be a great surprise if witnesses are produced who will say Rebecca told them she was going to "get" Zach because they broke up. Earlier the defense had Earp subpoenaed so they could call her as a defense witness. This happens sometimes, even though the witness may have already testified for the prosecution because the defense can question someone differently if that person is called as a defense witness rather than a prosecution witness.

Expect the defense to call on their experts to counter the testimony given by prosecution experts. They may produce forensic scientists or ballistics experts to give their opinion as to whether the wound to the skull was a gunshot wound or not. A defense expert may also have a different opinion about the caliber of the bullet. A forensic cell phone expert may give a different version of the "pings" or talk about some other pings that might be interesting from other phones or at other times. Rebecca Earp said Zach called her that morning on Dylan's phone and there might be some more information about that call. Experts might testify concerning the absence of any significant evidence on the gun. Question Document Examiners (handwriting experts) may address the handwriting on the note with Holly's name and address written on it.

Of course, the defense will do everything they legally can to discredit Jason Autry. The prosecution did a good job by sharing his background with the jury at the beginning of his testimony. The people on that jury understand real life and they know what they are dealing with in this case. I doubt they were shocked to find out the star witness is a career criminal and a drug addict. The state did a really good job of corroborating Autry's testimony. Having said that, if the defense can make the jury believe that Autry absolutely and unquestionably lied about even one significant fact, his entire testimony then comes into question.

The defense may also bring up the possibility that Autry was the killer and cooked up the story to get his immunity deal. By his own testimony, he puts himself all around the crime, but he didn't really "do" anything except ride in the truck and come up with ideas. His alibi is that he was at the wildlife refuge waiting to get in touch with Zach to buy some dope. The problem the defense has with this tactic is it puts their client awful close to admitting guilt. If Jason Autry committed this crime, from all the evidence presented, Zach Adams just about had to be there too. Cell phone records and the encounter with Dinsmore put the two together a lot that day.

Dope dealers and thugs tend to want to brag about what they have done. Whether what they say they have done is true or not is usually questionable. It would not be surprising if the defense produces witnesses who will testify Jason Autry said things about the case that differ from his courtroom testimony.

Another issue they may bring up is the possibility that someone else, besides those who have been mentioned in the trial, committed the murder. This was a huge investigation and there were many suspects and persons of interest developed. Investigators may have to explain how all those other suspects were eliminated.

Questions have already been asked about an affidavit TBI agents prepared to obtain a search warrant for financial records. In that document, it was alleged the family had given investigators false information. Autry's testimony brings methamphetamine into the picture when he said Adams said "they" went over there (the Bobo house) to teach Clint how to make meth. The same testimony describes Zach, Dylan, and Shayne all going to the house that morning. Clint says only one person was there. Of course, the other two could have been out of sight. If the prosecution has a good case, the defense may bring up things that will "muddy the water". They want to distract the jury and get the jurors to think about everything else but the real evidence.

There is always the possibility there may be questions about some of the victims' activities. If the defense uses this tactic, they must be cautious not to offend or alienate jurors.

The defense has notified the court they will call an alibi witness. It remains to be seen what kind of testimony that person may provide. The state knows who the alibi witness is and investigators probably have at least an idea of what the witness may say.

A big question is, will Zach or Dylan testify? Dylan does not have to defend himself in this case and his attorneys probably would advise him not to testify. Traditionally defense attorneys do NOT want to put their clients on the witness stand in a case of this nature. If the defendant gets on the witness stand it may open the door for the prosecution to ask about their prior criminal history and other things that the defense would rather the jury didn't hear. The defendant may make a bad impression on the jury by getting angry and exhibiting a violent demeanor or getting caught lying. Of course, if they can't shake the prosecution's case and discredit Autry's testimony, defense attorneys may feel they have no choice to put Adams on the stand to deny the allegations. The judge will instruct the jury that the defendant is not required to testify and the jury is not to hold it against him if he does not testify. It may still be hard for some jurors to accept the fact that a person who is not guilty would not stand up and deny the accusations. Defense attorneys must weigh all these factors in making their decision as to whether or not to put Zach Adams on the witness stand.

One thing that may come into play is the possibility of surprises. Sometimes a witness will testify to something totally unexpected. The witness could be making something up or they could have had heard something that jogged their memory since the last time they were questioned. In some instances, the right follow-up questions were not asked to elicit a complete answer from the witness. I was giving a deposition in a death penalty case and the defense attorneys asked if the killer had told me that he had hurt any other women. I answered, "Yes. He did." They didn't ask me what he said, so I didn't tell them. The same lawyers asked me the same question weeks later in federal appeals court and I responded, "Yes. He told me he had hurt many other women and he hurt them bad and he didn't give a dam how bad he hurt them and then he threw out of his car." This expanded answer caught the defense by surprise and they were very upset. I had done nothing wrong. I answered both questions truthfully. I have seen things like this happen many times. One job an investigator is responsible for is to try and make sure the prosecuting attorneys don't get surprised in court, but it happens.

BOBO CASE - THE PROSECUTION RESTS 9/20/17

On Monday 9/18, the prosecution produced its final witnesses before resting at 3:30 pm. The testimony included several associates of Zach Adams and each of them told of conversations they had with Adams in which he made incriminating statements concerning the death of Holly Bobo.

Adams' friend Anthony Phoenix said anytime Hollys' name came up Zach would get "sketchy and nervous". Phoenix describes a time when a group of friends was together and Hollys' disappearance was mentioned. Anthony says Zach became very upset and ran everybody out of the house. Once when the two men were riding around, Adams asked Phoenix if he wanted to go rape someone. On another occasion Adams told Phoenix, "I couldn't have picked a prettier b----." and "it was fun." Jason Autry quoted Adams using exactly the same words when he was describing what he had done to Holly.

Another friend, Jamie Darnell testified Adams showed him a knife and Adams told Darnell, "If you knew what that knife had done, he probably wouldn't want to hold it." It could be that a knife wound is what caused Holly to bleed. Autry said he saw blood on the blanket Holly was wrapped in and also saw some blood on Adams's truck.

Carl Stateler said he once heard Adams threaten a bartender by saying, "I'll do you like I did Holley Bobo". He also testified Adams told him, "I let Shayne hit it" and Darnell assumed he was talking about Holly.

There was also testimony from people who had been in jail with Zach Adams.

Adams saw Corey Rivers reading a Bible and began asking Rivers questions about forgiveness. Adams said he was in jail because of the disappearance of Holly Bobo and he was "there for the worst of it." He also told Rivers there was a video about Hollys' death and it was "right under the nose" of investigators working on the case.

Chris Swift testified Zach asked him if he thought God would forgive him for killing Holly Bobo.

Shawn Cooper said Adams asked him to tell Dylan Adams if he (Dylan) didn't keep quiet about Hollys' disappearance, he (Zach) would put Dylan "in the hole beside her." Another inmate, Jason Kirk, said he overheard this conversation.

Testimony was given by Decatur County dispatcher John Maxwell. He said on the night Holly disappeared, Zach Adams' grandfather called the dispatch center 3 times saying Zach was messed up on drugs and trying to get his brother's keys. Prior testimony would indicate Zach Adams might have needed transportation because he had hidden his truck at Victor Dinsmore's place. Police responded after the third call but no arrests were made.

The state called Terry Britt to the witness stand. Britt is a convicted rapist and was thoroughly investigated as a suspect in the disappearance of Holly Bobo. At one point Britt's phone was tapped and his house was bugged. Britt denied having anything to do with the disappearance and murder of Holly. TBI officials say Britt was cleared of having any involvement in the case.

THE BOBO TRIAL - THE DEFENSE 9/20/17

Former TBI agent Terry Dicus testified for the defense on Tuesday, the 8th day of the trial, and the theme of his testimony was that Terry Britt was responsible for the death of Holly

Bobo and that his investigation cleared Zach Adams. "I was wasting my time investigating these idiots." Dicus testified. He was referring to Adams, Autry, Austin, and Dylan Adams. He said cell phone pings showed Holly's phone was moving throughout the morning on the day she was abducted. He said at 8:17 am she was on her "home tower" and at 8:26 she was on the "next" tower. Dicus said he was focusing on people who did not have a good alibi. Zach Adams said he was at a gas station and a business in Parsons on the day Holly disappeared. No witnesses were called to corroborate this alibi. Dicus says he determined that Adams was not involved in the crime.

Dicus based his opinion of Britt's guilt on his history of sex offenses and the fact he lived near the Bobo home. Dicus also said Britt's alibi was "garbage. Britt said he and his wife had been involved in remodeling their home that day and had gone to a certain store to buy a bathtub. Dicus says no one at the store remembers anyone matching their description. He said Britt's voice was similar to a voice Clint heard and Britt may have changed his appearance after the abduction. During a search of Britt's home, it was discovered his computer contained videos depicting abduction and rape.   Cadaver dogs picked up scents of human decomposition on shovels, an ax, and a hammer near Britt's home, however, Dicus testified he didn't think the dogs were accurate. I have not heard any testimony indicating Holly's body was buried. Britt's phone was tapped and his home was bugged. He was never charged.

Under cross-examination, Dicus said he was not aware of any statements Adams had made regarding killing Holly Bobo. Dicus was removed from the case before Jason Autry began cooperating with the police. In rebuttal, the prosecution called former TBI Special Agent in Charge Jack Van Hooser to the stand. He testified he replaced Dicus as the TBI case agent because Dicus had lost his objectivity and developed "tunnel vision" regarding one particular suspect.

Deputy U.S. Marshall John Walker testified he interviewed Britt in jail as a favor to Agent Dicus. Walker did not advise Britt of his right to silence before the interview, even though Britt was in custody at the time of the interview. Walker said he did not read Britt his rights because he was not interviewing him to get testimonial evidence, but he asked Britt to tell him where Holly Bobo's body was located. It seems if Britt could reveal where Holly's body was located, that would have been a pretty good piece of evidence. Britt initially said he didn't recognize Holly's name and said he couldn't tell where the body was because he didn't *know* where the body was.

Part of Walker's testimony suggested that at one point in the interview, Britt offered to plead guilty to something (not clear exactly what) in reference to the murder. After Walker outlined his theory of what happened, Britt said, "Looks like you got it all figured out. I can just plead guilty and you can close the case." That statement could have been an offer to plead guilty or it could have been a sarcastic remark. Britt also allegedly asked how quickly he could get out of jail if he "gave" them something regarding the investigation.

On crossexamination, prosecution attorneys pointed out the fact that much of what Walker testified to was not in his report.

Dick Adams, the grandfather of Zach Adams, testified Dylan Adams was home in the bed when Dick Adams left the house that morning. He said he saw Dylan, Zach, and Shayne Austin on the interstate later that day. Mr. Adams explained he might be confused about some dates because he had lost his wife a couple of weeks before Holly's disappearance. He said he did not recall telling investigators they should "check all of Zach's friends."

Kristie Gutgsell was working with a bail bond company at the time of Holly's disappearance. She testified her company made bond for Zach Adams a week or so before Holly was abducted and when she saw him he had scratches. Whether these are the same scratches Rebecca Earp described and the FBI agent photographed two weeks later is a question the jury will debate.

Jonathan Reeves, president of JDR Telecom Solutions testified said Holly and Zach Adams phones were in separate places in Decatur County that morning from about 8:17 am until 9:10 am. Reeves said there were "stark differences" between his findings and those of TBI Agent Frizzell. He said his study showed Adams and Autry both being in the same sector of the Birdsong Tower at 9:50 am. That information agreed with Frizzell's testimony.

Zach Adams did not testify in his defense however the jury will be instructed by the judge this cannot be held against Adams.

The defense rested at the end of the day on Wednesday, the 9th day of the trial.

THE BOBO CASE - THE JURY   9/21/17

OK. The proof has been put on and both sides have made their closing arguments. The jury may have heard things that most of us did not. They also got a much better "look" at the witnesses than we did. As we pointed out in an earlier article, the jury's *perception* of what the truth is means more than anything, and about 2/3 of our communications process is governed by body language. The demeanor of the witness when he or she was testifying may determine how much the jury will believe that witness. This article will discuss some of the things the jurors may consider in their deliberations

In their first closing statement, the prosecution emphasized several things. The state detailed the horrible things that happened to Holly. One very important point that was emphasized was the testimony of two people who testified that Zach Adams told them he wasn't worried because the police did not have a gun. Adams made these statements before it was public knowledge that Holly was killed by a firearm as opposed to any other method. It was six months later after her remains were discovered before the manner of death was known. Zach already knew.

The defense attacked the government witnesses because of their criminal backgrounds. They said the prosecution case is full of holes. Zach Adams' attorneys say he is 100% innocent of the charges against him.

It is a given that Jason Autry is a low-life piece of you-know-what. You cannot "pick" your witnesses and get some with perfect backgrounds. People with perfect backgrounds don't tend to have a lot of information about terrible crimes.   When it comes down to it,

Jason is a snitch, and in a perfect world, if the story he tells is true, he should spend the rest of his life in prison or be executed. However, this is not a perfect world. The story that has been presented is that he helped dispose of the body and the others kidnapped, abused, and murdered Holley Bobo.

Am I sure that is the limit of his involvement? I am not convinced of that. It is a normal course of business for an informant to tell everything about everyone else, but maybe not be quite as forthcoming about what they have done themselves. Autry was given immunity in exchange for his testimony. He would have not have testified without a "deal", and without his cooperation, nobody gets prosecuted. Whether we should let one culprit go free in exchange for being able to prosecute another terrible person is a big question. The point is, that is the way it works in many instances.

When you have a "star" witness like Autry, you must do all you can to corroborate his testimony to give him some credibility because everybody automatically assumes he is lying. I thought Dinsmore was big in adding back-up to Autry. He verifies he hid Adams's truck and that he bought the gun by trading pills for it. He also verified the fight between Adams and Austin. An independent witness placed them all together that afternoon. Mr. Dick Adams says the night of Holly's disappearance, his grandson, Zach was messed up, which was probably not unusual, but he was also trying to get car keys. That could mean he was without transportation. Maybe Zach was without transportation because he was afraid to drive his truck and it was hidden at Dinsmore's. Autry said there was one shot fired and the forensic scientist agreed only one shot was fired. If I understood the testimony right, cell phone experts agreed that Autry and Adams were both hear the Birdsong cell phone tower at about the time Autry said they were there.

Last, but not least, we know why Autry gave this testimony. He cooperated to help himself and I will promise it was explained to him in no uncertain terms that if he was caught in a lie, all bets were off and he would be tried, at the least for accessory to first-degree murder.   I teach a lot of classes that discuss the use of informants. It is a necessary evil in the police business to deal with snitches. Even though the motive may be distasteful, if I know for sure why a person is giving information, I can work with it. Two of the most widely recognized motives that cause people to cooperate with police are money and gaining leniency for crimes the informant has committed. These are two of my favorite motives because I can easily understand them.

There was no real physical evidence. Neither the police, prosecutors nor defense attorneys can create evidence. They all must deal with what evidence they have and with a case that is years old, there usually is not much physical evidence left, especially when you don't even know where the main crime scene may be located! In the last few years, we have heard several stories about juries who acquitted a defendant because there was no DNA or fingerprint evidence. On CSI or Law and Order or some of those shows, they always have that type of evidence. Well, this is not a TV show or a movie and as I said before if the evidence is not there, it just isn't there. It does not at all mean the person who is being charged is not guilty, it only means that particular type of evidence was not present or recovered.

There are some other issues that I have questions about. Why did Zach Adams need Autry anyway if Zach, Dylan, and Shayne were already involved? Ordinarily, you want to limit the number of people that know you killed someone. One explanation would be that Autry was involved from the beginning. Another possible explanation was provided to me by a respected journalist friend of mine who has been in the courtroom throughout the trial. He said it was obvious Jason Autry was a "leader" in the group. He was bigger, smarter, and more sophisticated than the others involved. Also, according to Autry, Dylan Adams, Shayne Austin, and Zach Adams were tense and upset with one another. That might be another reason Zach needed Autry's help. Nobody else would have anything to do with it.

I also wonder about the gun. According to Autry's testimony, when he first saw the gun, it was on Shayne's side. Then it showed up on the floorboard in Zach's truck and was used to kill Holley. If Shayne and Zach were mad at one another, why would Shayne give Zach his gun? If everybody believed Holly was already dead, why did they need a gun in the truck? Maybe they planned to kill an officer if they were stopped with Holly's body in the truck.

The issue has been raised concerning Autry being able to review discovery material and make up his story according to what he learned about the case. It would seem he would have been able to make up a little better story if that was the case and removed himself further from any blame. If I had been him and I was making up a story, I would have said something like, "Zach tricked me into coming to the house that morning and then stuck a gun in my face and told me if I didn't help him, he would kill me."

It was very coincidental that two separate witnesses, Autry and Phoenix, quote Zach Adams using exactly the same words when describing what he had done to Holly. We know of no reasonable way these two witnesses could have gotten together and made up this statement. I believe Zach Adams used these words, "I couldn't have picked a prettier b----. It was fun."

There has been much discussion about Clint Bobo's description of the person who abducted his sister. Eye witness testimony was once considered to be some of the best evidence you could have. In recent years eye witness testimony has come under attack, in large part due to the number of people imprisoned due to eye witness evidence and then later being proved to be innocent.   A couple of things that can distort a witness's description are sensory overload and confabulation. Sensory overload can occur when so much happens in a short amount of time, the brain basically cannot absorb all the data correctly. Receiving the original information is the first step in memory and recollection and if it is not done properly, it messes up the entire process. A whole lot of stuff happened in a short amount of time in Clint's situation and he could have been somewhat overwhelmed. Confabulation is a psychiatric term describing the production of fabricated, distorted, or misinterpreted memories *without* the intention to deceive. In Clint's case, this would mean if he thought the man he saw leaving with Holly was her boyfriend, his brain might make the interpretation that the description of the person Clint saw should match the description of the boyfriend. Another thing that can alter the accuracy of a witness's description is when the witness tries to be *too helpful* and provides more detail than they are truly capable of doing. They are trying to be helpful and also they may feel if they don't provide a lot of information, they will appear to be uncooperative or dumb.

The Dicus, Britt, Walker thing is confusing to me. There was a lot of time spent investigating Mr. Britt and it produced no evidence at all. Wiretaps are rare and electronic surveillance (bugging) of a residence is almost unheard of in rural west Tennessee. The only testimony I reviewed that appeared to put the spotlight on Britt was the fact that he has been convicted of sex crimes and he lived somewhere in the area of Holly Bobo's home. I wonder how many convicted sex offenders lived within a 50 mile radius of Holly? A lot, I bet. I also wonder how Dicus concluded that whoever abducted Holly Bobo was a sexual predator. He knew she left her home in the company of an unknown person and her personal items were found strewn around the countryside. That was about all that was really known for sure until her remains were found. I don't see how you take that information and decide a single sexual predator is responsible for what happened to the victim. Walker's interview of Britt is also confusing. He went to interview a man in jail and the reason he is interviewing this guy is because the TBI case agent believes the inmate is the prime suspect in the disappearance and probable murder of a young woman. Walker says he did not interview to get testimonial evidence, but the questions he is asking are about finding the remains of Holly Bobo. Sounds like evidence to me. It seems

321

obvious when Britt offered to plead
guilty so they could close the case, he
was being a smart aleck. I believe if
anybody involved thought Britt was
genuinely talking about making a plea
bargain, which would have to include
making a confession, investigators and
prosecutors would have been all over it.

I think former TBI SAC Jack Van
Hooser was correct when he described
Dicus as having tunnel vision. It is
fortunate Van Hooser finally was placed
in charge of the case.

Former State Attorney General
Paul G. Summers first explained the
K.I.S.S. (keep it simple stupid) method
to me when I was a young TBI agent. It
is a great principle to follow when
investigating a criminal case.

#1 simple thing.   Zach told an FBI
agent that he went to a gas station and
a business in Parsons that morning. It
strains belief to think he was running
around Parsons that morning and didn't
see someone he knew. He is well known
in the area. If his story is true, why

didn't we see someone get on the witness stand and say Zach Adams couldn't have kidnapped Holly Bobo because I saw him at the service station that morning?

#2 simple thing. Without Jason Autry's testimony, it appears there is no prosecutable case. That's why the state had to work out a deal with him. If Autry and his attorney reviewed the discovery material, it seems like they should have seen that all Jason had to do was keep his mouth shut. Shayne Austin can't testify and apparently neither can Zach Adams or Dylan Adams.

THE BOBO TRIAL - THE VERDICT

On 9/22/17 a Hardin County Tennessee convicted Zach Adams on all 8 counts relating to the kidnapping, rape, and murder of Holly Bobo. The next day he was allowed to receive a sentence of life in prison with no possibility of parole plus 50 years. He agreed to plea so the prosecution would not pursue the death penalty.

Zach Adams asked for a new trial citing the lack of evidence and the location of the trial. The trial was in Hardin County Tennessee which is an adjoining county to Decatur County where the murder occurred. In all, the defense presented 56 reasons Adams should be granted a new trial. In August of 2020, the request was denied.

John Dylan Adams entered an Alford plea in the Bobo case and he will serve 15 years for one count of facilitation of first-degree murder and 35 years for especially aggravated kidnapping. The sentences will run concurrently. An Alford plea allows a defendant to enter a plea of guilty without admitting guilt.

Jason Autry finished his sentence in federal prison for firearms violations and was released in September of 2020.

In December Of 2020 Autry was arrested in Benton County Tennessee on charges of possession of drugs, possession of a weapon, and evading arrest. A week later he was also indicted in federal court for being a felon in possession of a firearm.

THE GOLDEN STATE KILLER

The case of The Golden State Killer is one of the most interesting ever. There is a tremendous amount of information about the killer and the cases and at times, one media source conflicts with another. I spent a lot of time sifting through information and trying to organize the facts in a way that would cover the most pertinent points and at the same time be easy to "put together". Hopefully, I did a good job.

A person doesn't just wake up one morning and decide to be a serial killer! Becoming a serial murderer is an evolutionary process.

Authorities believe the same person may have committed up to 120 burglaries in the Visalia region between 1974 and 1976. Investigators further theorize the same guy may be responsible for 50 rapes and 13 murders beginning in 1976 and lasting until 1987.

In all, 10 counties in the state of California were involved.

Of course, media came up with nicknames such as The Visalia Ransacker, The East Area Rapist, The Original Nightstalker (Richard Ramirez was called *The Nightstalker)*, and The Golden State Killer.

The Visalia Ransacker

A prolific burglar appears to have begun his career in the Visalia California area in 1974. His strange patterns and the sheer number of burglaries earned the burglar the nickname the *Visalia Ransacker*.

The *Ransacker* was known to invade numerous houses in the same neighborhood and hit different homes on consecutive nights.

In sort of a unique twist, the burglar placed dishes in front of the door to serve as an alarm if someone came in the house while he was doing his business. This peculiar tactic was later seen to be used in the attacks of The East Area Rapist as well as The Golden State Killer.

In at least one incident he broke into the same house on different nights. The first time he stole the wife's underwear and jewelry but the second time he broke in, nothing was *determined* to be missing. It is possible the burglar took something of little or no value, but the homeowners didn't miss anything.

Numerous burglaries with nothing of value taken should cause an investigator's antennas to go up! The burglar may be searching for items he has a fetish for such as women's undergarments, shoes, cosmetics, jewelry, etc... These things could be necessary for the burglar to act out some type of fantasy or they might be considered souvenirs.

The Ransacker was known to leave women's garments lying around the home and stealing such things as Piggy Banks, earrings (sometimes only one earring), and personal photographs. He also left semen at the crime scene. These characteristics were consistent with The East Area Rapist as well as The Golden State Killer.

During this time period, one woman in the neighborhood of the burglaries discovered shoe prints in her yard and the fence gate was left open. This could have been The Ransacker "casing" her home. However, it could have been something else that had nothing to do with a burglary! People were scared and maybe a little paranoid while all these burglaries were taking place. Gun sales were up because homeowners were arming themself. There were fewer home burglaries during The Ransacker's career as a burglar because the "normal" burglars were afraid they might get shot breaking into someone's home.

In another possibly related occurrence, homeowners in the same neighborhood found messages written with body fluids on their bedroom window. If this was The Ransacker, and it probably was, it shows an escalation in his attempts to frighten and intimidate.

One woman in the area received silent hang-up telephone calls at 8 p.m. every night for a week. Once again, The Ransacker enjoyed scaring people and considered the use of fear as one form of dominance.

It appeared as though The Ransacker liked to utilize drainage ditches and river levees to sneak up on his victims.

The East Area Rapist

Sacramento County suffered almost four dozen rapes from 1976 - 1979. The sexual predator was dubbed the *East Area Rapist*.

Similar to The Ransacker, apparently The Rapist "cased" his victim's homes before his attacks.

In one case a thirteen year old girl was raped and just a few blocks away a woman was raped while her husband was forced to watch. Once again this is similar to The Ransacker's pattern of committing multiple crimes in the same area.

In March of 1978, a homeowner noticed the lock on his garage door had been broken. Two days later his home was broken into. The Rapist made the man's wife tie the homeowner up. The Rapist then sexually assaulted the wife while the husband helplessly looked on.

A man woke up in his home and attacked an intruder who was standing at the foot of his bed. The wife ran out of the house while the two men were struggling. Then the husband ran out of the house. Consistent with the East Area Rapist's M.O., once he lost control, he ran away. This incident in Danville in July 1979, is believed to be The Rapist's last crime in northern California.

In October 1979 The Rapist appeared in Santa Barbara, attacking a couple in their home. After being tied up, the woman somehow got loose and ran out of the house. The Rapist caught her, brought the lady back into the house, and tied her up again. While all this was taking place, the man of the house freed himself and ran into the backyard screaming for help. Once again the attacker ran away once he was no longer in control!

The Rapist was also known to disable lights and in some instances hide any weapons in the home that might be used against him. Studying the victim's residence before the crime so that lights and locks can be disabled shows intensive planning. These activities mirror characteristics of The Golden State Killer as well as The Original Nightstalker.

The Rapist jumped off roofs and jumped over fences to evade capture showing a great deal of athleticism.

Total Domination

Not only did he seek dominance by using ligatures, but he also used fear to maintain control. He enjoyed blinding his victims by shining a flashlight in their eyes. It was also common for him to stick a gun in their face. On one occasion when a victim showed no fear, the rapist became furious and viciously raped her anally.

In one instance involving a man and woman couple, after the intruder tied them up, he carried the woman into the kitchen. When he went into another room, she heard him say, 'I gotta kill them". He said it about a dozen times. The female managed to get loose and she tried to run away, but he caught her. In the confusion, the man freed himself and escaped. Once the would-be rapist realized he had lost control, he stole a bicycle and left.

The Rapist was known to tell victims not to look at him or make any movements whatsoever and threatened to kill them if they did not follow all of his commands.

The First Murders

While still functioning as a burglar/rapist he demonstrated his willingness to kill. These first murders were probably more an act of self-defense than part of a serial killer's personality.

On September 11, 1975, a college professor, Claude Snelling was shot and killed trying to rescue his daughter from an abductor. The description and M.O. of the abductor matched the Ransacker. Ballistics matched the murder weapon to a gun that was stolen in a burglary that was tied to the Visalia Ransacker. When faced with resistance, the coward kicked the young girl a couple of times and ran away.

In Cordova Meadows, in 1978, pre-cut ropes were found at the scene of a homicide. It appeared as though the victims, who were walking their dog, had surprised a prowler and the prowler killed them both. It was believed in the excitement the prowler dropped the ropes by mistake. The East Area Rapist was known to bring pre-cut ropes to his crimes. This incident was the first time The Rapist committed murder, but it may have been a defensive act.

In 1979 in Rancho Cordova, the burglar/rapist attacked a couple in their home. The man resisted strongly and was killed with a pistol. The intruder then shot the woman in the head, execution-style. The victims were tied up and the bindings were the same as those used by the rapist in his other crimes. There were also shoe impressions that matched those from other crime scenes. The killer escaped on a stolen bicycle. The behavior fit a profile that had become all too familiar.

He enjoyed killing.

The Serial Killer

Beginning in 1980 there were a series of murders in southern California continuing until 1986. Investigation indicated the same murderer was responsible for them. The media initially named the killer *The Original Nightstalker*. He would eventually be known as *The Golden State Killer*. The victims were shot and/or beaten to death. The final known victim was an 18 year old woman who was raped and bludgeoned to death. In some of the murders, husbands and boyfriends were also killed.

As the seriousness of his attacks increased, the crimes began to be committed less frequently. As a burglar and rapist, he acted out about every two weeks, but, once he became a killer, he only killed a couple of times a year. Maybe he was becoming afraid of being caught. Perhaps the murders gratified him for a longer period of time. Maybe he was just getting older.

In March 1980, in Ventura, it became evident the rapist had become a full-blown killer. He attacked a married couple in their home. He tied them up, sexually assaulted the women, and then beat them both to death with a log he got from the backyard. A log was quieter than a gun, but probably more important to the killer, it was an up close and personal way to kill. To the murderer, it was the epitome of dominance and sadism.

In February 1981, a lady returned home after visiting her husband in the hospital. The killer was waiting for her. He tied her up, sexually assaulted her, and beat her to death. He covered her with blankets before bludgeoning her and in a new twist, he untied her and carried the ligatures with him when he left. Evidently, he figured out police could use the ropes as evidence to identify him.

In 1982, one of his victims got a phone call at her work, she believes the call was from the person she knew as The East Area Rapist. The lady was not working at the place he called when he attacked her. Maybe he ran into her accidentally. She had no idea how he knew she was working there. It terrified her. Fortunately, she never heard from him again.

A Santa Barbara couple was beaten to death. The man tried to fight the killer and was shot in the face. The woman was raped.

The last known murder The Golden State Killer committed was in May of 1986 in Irvine. It had been 5 years since he had killed. At the time of the attack the victim, Janelle Cruz, was staying alone in the house. She told a friend she had a feeling she was being watched. On the night of her death, she left home at about 10:30 pm and was gone for 15 minutes. It is not known where she went. When she returned, the killer was waiting for her inside the home. Evidence at the scene indicated she resisted her attacker. She was raped and viciously bludgeoned to death. She was beaten so badly, the casket remained closed at her funeral.

The last two victims of the Golden State Killer, including Ms. Cruz, lived in houses that were listed for sale.

Investigators believe the murderer may have attended "open houses" at both places and either disabled or removed window locks. The Visalia Ransacker was known to have used this tactic also. It is not known if the victims were targeted and followed to the residence or if the residence itself was targeted because it provided easy access. Once inside, he would have been able to see photographs of those who lived there and decide if someone who fit his victim profile lived there.

In the latter part of his career, it seems many victims were able to escape. Was he getting tired or just getting sloppy. Maybe the excitement of trying to capture the victim after an escape attempt was part of a new fantasy the killer was enjoying.

What kind of person would do these things?

The crime scenes rarely produced fingerprints or trace evidence.

Eventually, the rapist/killer began to remove evidence, such as the rope he used to bind his victims. It is unclear if he developed these tactics because of media reports or because of his police training.

In many instances, he used weapons of opportunity so the weapon would not lead police back to him. A weapon of opportunity is one that is already at the crime scene such as a log or a sprinkler head.

It seemed to be common for the killer to tie the victim's hands and feet and at times he would use torn sheets to bind and gag his victims. Victims were tied with their hands behind their back with the same kind of knot, a "diamond knot".

It is clear ligatures were a strong part of his fantasy. The tying, binding, and gagging were part of his overall effort to dominate. As mentioned earlier, on several other occasions when it seemed a victim might overpower the rapist/killer, he would either run away or resort to using a gun.

Dominance, Control, Fear, and Sadism

The offender's desire to be in control and totally dominate the situation can be seen in his normal method of operation.
Below are some of the things the killer is known to have said to victims.
He threatened to cut the nipples off of a woman's breast and cut her fingers off if she made noise.
"You want me to cut off your ear?"
"I will slit your throat"
"I will kill your kids and bring their ears to you"
In the midst of one attack, the killer began sobbing said "mommy I don't want to do this anymore". Was this an expression of some specific type of mental disorder or just an act? Maybe

he was trying to point investigators in the wrong direction by giving the *impression* he was schizophrenic. If the police believed this, they have targeted their suspect search only toward people with a history of schizophrenia. Maybe he was suffering from schizophrenia. He may also have been just toying with the victim and making them even more fearful.

How could he be identified?

A total of 3 sketches were made from witness/victim descriptions. All 3 depicted white males and most described him as having an athletic build, and this would seem to fit the offender. Many of the things he did when committing his crimes took a certain degree of physical dexterity. Jumping off roofs, running, walking through drainage ditches, fighting, etc...

It must be considered some of the sketches were produced from witnesses describing *someone acting strangely in the area*. It may not have been the killer at all!

Just because a possible suspect doesn't look like a composite drawing does NOT mean the person should automatically be dismissed as a suspect. Investigators must consider ALL the information they know.

Sketches and composite drawings can be good or bad depending on the witness and the opportunity to view the suspect. Of course, if the bad guy is wearing a mask, as this suspect was, it makes a good identification even harder.

Jackson Tn. Police Detective Roy Towater produced a composite drawing of a child predator killer named Robert Glen Coe that was so accurate a relative called the day the drawing showed up in the paper and gave the person's name. Coe later confessed.

The Golden State Killer seemed to be familiar with guns. If he found guns at the victim's home, he would unload the weapons. The killer also brought a gun with him to commit his crimes.

He used military lingo and wore military-type clothing.

Many times we get caught up with how a suspect *looks*. Investigators must remember such things a manner of speech and even smell can help identify someone. A young child who was blindfolded while her mother was tortured told us the man had a strong smell of gasoline about him. We never solved the case, but one of the prime suspects ran a "chop shop operation". He would buy stolen cars, "chop" them up and sell the parts. Obviously, he might smell like gasoline!

Media Influence

The predator enjoyed media attention, especially when the news emphasized his power to dominate, and inflict pain.

An individual with the characteristics he exhibited might keep copies of newspapers and perhaps tape newscasts. Keep in mind he was proud of what he had done and would enjoy reliving the experience in his mind. Reviewing media reports and looking at or fondling souvenirs and memorabilia he kept from the crime scene or victim could add realism to his recollections.

On one occasion a news report speculated the killer would not attack a location if there was a man present. After that report aired, The Golden State Killer seemed to begin to prefer situations when men were present and seemed to go out of his way to dominate the men. He was essentially saying, "I'll show YOU!"

At an awareness meeting presented by a local sheriff's department, an attendee voiced his opinion that no single person should be able to overpower 2 or more people. A few weeks later the man who spoke up at the meeting was found murdered along with his wife in their home. The murder was so brutal the casket was closed at the funeral. Another example of, "I'll show YOU!"

It is possible the media could be useful when dealing with an offender who is concerned with his public image. Perhaps the killer could be tricked into showing up at a certain place or something of this nature.

Some type of comment in the media might a predictable response that could help identify him. It would be wise to consult with the experts at the FBI Behavioral Science Unit to determine what should be said.

Using the media can be tricky. Investigators do not want to make the situation worse or cause someone to be harmed.

The abduction and murder of Holly Bobo in rural western Tennessee was a very high profile crime. The victim had recently graduated from a very small high school and in an effort to produce leads, two pages from her high school annual were shown in the area's most widely circulated newspaper. She was an attractive white girl with long blond hair. There were two other girls shown in the annual who looked similar to the victim. If her murderer had been the right type of killer, showing pictures of someone with physical characteristics that were similar to Holly could have introduced the murderer to another victim.

The FBI Profile

In 2016 the FBI announced a $50,000 reward for information leading to the *arrest and conviction* of the person known as The Golden State Killer.

The FBI also released their ideas as to what characteristics the killer possessed. The FBI said he was probably a white male, about 6 feet tall with blond or light brown hair, and an athletic build. They went on to say the murderer had an interest in or had received training in the military or law enforcement and an affinity for firearms.

How did the DNA evidence surface?

Investigators put together data from several old crime scene evidence samples, such as semen, and created a genetic profile of the unknown suspect. They then uploaded THAT generic profile to GEDmatch for comparison with their database of 650,000 genetically profiles. GEDmatch is a private company developed by the Mormon Church to share genealogical information and assist in locating missing or unknown family members.

The GEDmatch program indicated a group of relatives that shared some of the same genetic characteristics as the generic profile the police had submitted.

After receiving the positive report from GEDmatch, the investigators did some good, old fashion, basic police work to move the case forward. They looked at the group and used the facts they had gathered in all the cases they believed were connected. These facts were used to "rule out" potential suspects using such things as age, location, death, etc... For example, if the crime was committed on April 4th, 1987, and a possible suspect, Joe Blow, was in Argentina, Joe gets ruled out. He couldn't have been the perpetrator. After a whole bunch of work, they were able to exclude everybody in the group, except 72 year old James Joseph DeAngelo.

At that point, they set up surveillance on DeAngelo. Following him, in his day-to-day activities, the investigators were able to get useable DNA samples by retrieving things he discarded. You could say "trash" caught the Golden State Killer!

The DNA testing comparing these samples produced a positive "Hit".

A tremendous amount of good police work had already been done on these cases. That work, combined with the efforts put forth after the "Hit", gave meaning to the DNA evidence to make prosecutable cases.

Who is James Joseph DeAngelo?

DeAngelo's mother was a waitress and his father was a welder.

The accused killer, originally from New York, was a Navy veteran and served 2 years in Vietnam.

In 1973 he became a police officer with the Exeter California Police Department which is located about midway between Sacramento and Los Angeles. He was 27 years old.

In 1976 DeAngelo went to work for the Auburn California Police Department about 75 miles from Sacramento.

According to media reports, in 1979, DeAngelo was cited for shoplifting a hammer and some dog repellent. These items could be tools to help him commit his disgusting crimes. Perhaps instead of buying these items, he enjoyed the thrill of stealing them. When approached concerning these minor thefts, he became very emotional and put up a fight.

DeAngelo was eventually convicted of shoplifting, placed on probation fined one hundred dollars, and eventually fired from the police department. Some have theorized the reason The Golden State Killer was able to evade capture for so long was because he had been a police officer, therefore the police were covering up for him. Let's see, he got fired for shoplifting, but caught a break for rape and murder?? Right.

In 1973 the killer got married and the marriage produced three daughters and several grandchildren. He and his wife separated several years before his arrest. Most of the time those who have the personality profile of a serial killer do not have personal relations lasting very long. Their human relations skills are not the greatest, as might be expected.

In recent years DeAngelo worked as a mechanic in a warehouse and was described by co-workers as a "regular Joe". He retired in 2017 and declared he was going to "do a lot of fishing".

Even though he and his wife were separated, some of his children and grandchildren lived with him. It is sort of "outside the norm" for a serial killer's children and grandchildren to move in with him, however, people with this type of personality profile are known to be good actors when they want to be!

Neighbors are quoted as saying he kept his lawn in "meticulous" condition.

The killer drew permanent lines on his driveway to make sure he parked his boat in the right position.

DeAngelo is said to have had anger problems for decades. Once, in 1994, in a dispute involving a barking dog, he threatened to "deliver a load of death" to his neighbor.

He was known to throw temper tantrums over such things as losing his keys. Acquaintances say he calmed down in the last few years.

DeAngelo was arrested at his home. He told police he had a roast in the oven. The officers told him they would take care of the roast.

Why did the murders stop in 1987? Maybe he reached the level where the killings didn't satisfy his needs. Perhaps he discovered another way to achieve gratification. It is possible his physical condition prevented him from engaging in intense physical activity.

We will never know for sure.

Key Issues

- 85 burglaries and the Claude Snelling murder were linked to Visalia Ransacker. His plea of guilty to the murder of Claude Snelling confirmed he was the Visalia Ransacker.

- M.O. and common characteristics relate The Rapist and The Ransacker to one another. In 2001 DNA matches linked the rapes to the murders, linking The Golden State Killer to The East Area Rapist and The Visalia Ransacker.
- There is no mention of DNA work on the burglaries. When the burglaries were taking place, no one knew anything about DNA. Evidence was collected differently back then and there was no thought of having it tested for DNA 20 years down the road.
- Some commonalities in the California crimes
  - The offender wore a ski mask.
  - A military-type knot (diamond knot) was used to tie the victims.
  - The perpetrator liked to use stolen bicycles to escape.
  - He regularly took items from the crime scene and seemed to have a special affinity for jewelry, coins, guns, piggy banks,

women's undergarments, and victim's identification.

- When footprints were found at crime scenes, a similar size 9 shoe print was found.
- The subject was consistently described as being of medium height, athletic build, and sporting medium length brown hair.
- The use of dishes as alarms. Some characteristics carry more weight than others, depending on how unique the particular characteristic may be. This one is VERY unusual, and therefore lends, considerable credibility to the theory the same person committed all these crimes. You may also notice an evolution in the way this alarm system was used. At first, dishes were set up in the doorways to let the intruder know if the homeowner had returned home. As the offender develops toward more

serious crimes, the dishes were placed on a victim who was tied up. If the rapist/killer heard the dishes rattle, he knew the tied-up victim was trying to get loose! The "dish alarm" system was known to be used by The Visalia Ransacker, The East Area Rapist, and The Golden State Killer.

- In cases of multiple murders in different counties, California law has a provision saying ALL of the murders may be prosecuted in any county that was the site of one of the killings. Of course, investigators and prosecutors must show convincing evidence that the murders are related.
- The statute of limitations had run out on the rapes and burglaries, so they could not be prosecuted. DeAngelo admitted guilt to many of them. There is no statute of limitations on murder.

- DNA matches tied DeAngelo to 8 murders. He pleaded guilty to 13 murders in all and ended up with 12 consecutive life sentences plus 8 years.

DeAngelo fits a commonly observed behavioral profile of an organized serial killer. The offender's crimes may be a means to achieve some sort of sexual gratification by acting out his fantasies. The crimes typically begin with burglaries or maybe arson fires. Most people remember the serial killer David Berkowitz, *The Son of Sam* killer, because of his murders but he was also known to have set dozens of arson fires. After a while, these acts "get old" and don't provide the *rush* this individual is trying to achieve so he progresses to sexual assaults.

When he reaches the point where rape doesn't provide the gratification he seeks, he may then turn into a full-blown serial killer. The acts of violence committed by these monsters are unbelievably vicious and may include bondage, cannibalism, decapitation, sadism, torture, and of course, complete dominance and control.

Some others who had multiple kills offered excuses for their behavior when I questioned them.

Kenneth O'Guin said he would pick up girls in clubs and take them out. At some point, in his warped mind, the girl became his wife, whom he said had been unfaithful to him. He would, "hurt them, and hurt them bad, and didn't care how bad he hurt them". Eventually, he confessed to killing five girls. O'Guin died on Death Row in Tennessee.

When questioned about killing an infant, Tommy Lynn Sells said, "sometimes the knife just goes crazy". Sells was convicted of killing 23 people and was executed by the State of Texas.

The cowardly Golden State Killer killer copied this ploy because he didn't have the courage to live up to the consequences of his actions.

DeAngelo had to appear in court to enter guilty pleas to the murders and some of the rapes he committed. The evidence of his guilt was overwhelming. He was sentenced to multiple terms of life without parole.

He couldn't simply deny what he had done, but he didn't have the guts to accept the responsibility for his actions, so he tried to shift the blame. The murderer said an inner personality named "Jerry" forced him to commit the crimes. DeAngelo went on to say, "I didn't have the strength to push him (Jerry) out. I didn't want to do those things, he made me. I mean, he was a part of me. I pushed Jerry out and I had a happy life."

Thanks to all of those who had the dedication and compassion for others to stick with it until justice was served.

About The Author

Jim Leach

Mr. Leach began his law enforcement career in 1975 as an officer with the Safety and Security Department at the University of Tennessee at Martin. He then accepted a position as a patrol officer with the Sharon Tennessee Police Department. Following his work at Sharon PD, he was privileged to serve as a Trooper with the Tennessee Highway Patrol.

Mr. Leach started his investigative career as a Special Agent with the Tennessee Bureau of Investigation where he specialized in the investigation of violent crime, official corruption, narcotics, and undercover work of all types. He was known for working with other agencies, state, local, and federal, and served on numerous task forces. Some of his most notable cases involved serial killers and other capital murders cases, large interstate narcotics investigations, and working undercover solicitation cases involving multiple murders.

Leach was promoted to Special Agent in Charge with the TBI and placed in charge of 53 counties east of Nashville. He supervised 27 criminal investigators working major felony cases.

In the latter part of 1988, he was appointed Director of the Criminal Investigation Division for the Tennessee Department of Safety, commonly known as the THP CID. During his tenure, the division grew from 45 members to 150 and expanded their duties to investigate any type crime of that that occurred in the state from follow-up investigations on felony traffic stops, to narcotics investigations, to murder cases and everything in between. The division also handled any serious internal investigations in the department.

Mr. Leach served as a cold case homicide investigator for the Jackson Tennessee Police Department, the Gibson Tennessee County Sheriff Department, and the Madison County Tennessee Sheriff Department. Since 1994 he has been co-owner of Training Services Group Inc. along with his partner Commander Dennis Mays. Along with their associates, they have provided training in law enforcement, homeland security, workplace violence, and personal safety training to thousands of students throughout the United States.

Mr. Leach is a graduate of the FBI National Academy (133rdSession), the Tennessee Government Executive Institute, and holds a B.S. degree from UT Martin. He was the Tennessee representative to the first Arkansas Leader seminar presented by the F.B.I. and the University of Arkansas Little Rock and the S.T.A.R. (small town and rural drug enforcement) training seminar at the Federal Law Enforcement Training Center in Glynco Georgia.

He served as the vice president of the Tennessee Narcotics Officers Association and in 2003 received the award for Outstanding Achievement from the University of Tennessee Martin.

Mr. Leach has conducted security assessments for many banks, schools, and businesses and helped them to develop effective security policies and procedures.

After writing numerous articles for various publications discussing workplace violence, personal safety, and homeland security, Mr. Leach published his first book, "You Can Tell ME". The work is intended to be a simple guide for effective interviewing and is available on Amazon.com in both paperback and Kindle versions. He just finished his second book, "Not in OUR

HOUSE" which deals with defeating workplace violence, and his third book, "Simply Safer, provides effective tips to keep you safer in your everyday life. Jim appears weekly as a law enforcement analyst on Steve Bowers' popular radio show "Blue Suede Forever" and hosts his own show, along with co-host Brad McCoy, *The Investigator*. Both shows can be heard on 93.1 FM in Jackson Tennessee and they stream live on "www.the talk of jackson.com.

Mr. Leach was inducted into the Carroll County Tennessee Sports Hall of Fame in 2019.

To review more of his work, you can find many podcasts, blogs, and articles at "tugnews.com",and Facebook page "Tennessee Underground".

www.ingramcontent.com/pod-product-compliance
Lightning Source LLC
Chambersburg PA
CBHW072108270326
41931CB00010B/1488